EMPOWERED: A WOMAN FACULTY OF COLOR'S
GUIDE TO TEACHING AND THRIVING

TEACHING, ENGAGING, AND THRIVING IN HIGHER ED

James M. Lang and Michelle D. Miller, SERIES EDITORS

EMPOWERED: A WOMAN FACULTY OF COLOR'S GUIDE TO TEACHING AND THRIVING

CHAVELLA T. PITTMAN

University of Oklahoma Press : Norman

Library of Congress Control Numbers:
(hardcover) 2024060630
(paperback) 2025001821

ISBN: 978-0-8061-9564-3 (hardcover)
ISBN: 978-0-8061-9565-0 (paperback)

Empowered: A Woman Faculty of Color's Guide to Teaching and Thriving is Volume 7 in the Teaching, Engaging, and Thriving in Higher Ed series.

Copyright © 2025 by Chavella T. Pittman. Published by the University of Oklahoma Press, Norman, Publishing Division of the University. Manufactured in the U.S.A.

The views and opinions expressed herein are solely those of the individual author(s) and do not reflect the policy, opinions, or positions of the University of Oklahoma, its regents, officers, or employees.

The paper in this book meets the guidelines for permanence and durability of the Committee on Production Guidelines for Book Longevity of the Council on Library Resources, Inc. ∞

The manufacturer's authorized representative in the EU for product safety is Mare Nostrum Group B.V., Mauritskade 21D, 1091 GC Amsterdam, The Netherlands, email: gpsr@mare-nostrum.co.uk.

All rights reserved. No part of this publication may be reproduced, stored in a retrieval system, or transmitted, in any form or by any means, electronic, mechanical, photocopying, recording, or otherwise—except as permitted under Section 107 or 108 of the United States Copyright Act—without the prior written permission of the University of Oklahoma Press. To request permission to reproduce selections from this book, write to Permissions, University of Oklahoma Press, 2800 Venture Drive, Norman OK 73069, or email rights.oupress@ou.edu.

CONTENTS

Introduction (Read This First)	1
How to Use This Book	9
1. Establish the High Ground	12
2. Anchor to Strong Points	38
3. Build a Protective and Nurturing Bubble	62
4. They Don't "Get It" (and That's Not Required)	85
5. Remain Authentic (and Innovative)	111
6. Create Joy Despite Everything	134
Appendix: For Allies	165
Acknowledgments	175
Suggestions for Further Resources	179
Notes	183
Index	209

INTRODUCTION
(Read This First)

It is possible to have the academic career of your dreams—for real!

Though history and research show that teaching obstacles frequently sink the careers of women faculty of color, that's because the problem has gone without a go-to resource for combating that in a hands-on way.

Good news: You've just found that resource.

USE THIS BOOK to protect your teaching, empower your career, and (re)claim your joy!

Hey fellow woman of color!

I'm so excited you're here! At the risk of coming on strong right from page one, I have a promise to offer you. I know, we barely know each other yet, but I promise that if you read, and use even a few of the action steps in this book, you'll be far less stressed, and far more empowered than you've ever been as an academic. Do I have your attention so far?

Now, what exactly do I mean by "empowered," you ask? Good question. We're going to get into the challenges you're facing today in a bit, but first let's go on a little imaginative journey together to explore the word empowered.

For just a few moments, let's think about your campus. Bring it into your mind's eye, except, let's set our imagination free. Instead of thinking about how your campus is today, imagine your campus in the future, not too far from now. As a woman faculty of color, this future campus is such a nourishing place that . . .

. . . you're birthing a bounty of intellectual ideas. You fully and freely pursue, investigate, teach, and disseminate these ideas in this version of your campus. Ahh! Beautiful. Furthermore . . .

. . . your academic freedom is not only protected on your campus, but it is protected so well, it has become an example for other campuses. Ideas that have historically had less airtime, you're giving them their day in the sun.

. . . you're rightfully renewed, tenured and/or promoted for your innovative and positive contributions to scholarship, service, and teaching. But that's not all.

Your future campus is a haven of safety for all folks of color—faculty, staff, students, and leaders. You and the folks on campus who look like you are thriving on all levels—physically, emotionally, economically, and mentally.

That's what I call a vision worth having! Now, let me ask you. How do you imagine you'd feel in that scenario? If you said "empowered," that's it. That's IT. THAT is what I mean when I say empowered. This book is about you being more empowered than you've ever been in your academic career.

Now you're probably wondering, "How do I make this vision a reality?" Or, you may be thinking, "I really want to get beyond surviving, and thrive, like in that imagination exercise." Or, you might be stepping in as a relatively new academic.

All good! An important part of creating a vision like this is to focus on what you want, as much as or more than what you don't want. When was the last time you allowed yourself to dream of what's possible—what you most want for your campus life and academic career?

I hope you said "Dr. Pittman, I just did it one minute ago two paragraphs above" (though you can just call me Chavella). If you did say that, YES, that is the spark I'm talking about, and while we will cover a lot of challenges in all seriousness in this book, we're going to do it with our senses of humor intact. All the more so if the humor is dry, wry, or even slightly searing! This is going to be a truth-telling, no-holds barred, and above all action-oriented experience.

Woman Faculty of Color—I See You

Before moving on, there's something important I want to make plain. I wrote this book explicitly for women faculty of color—you. I want you to know that I SEE you and am talking directly to you. Hey y'all! :)

This book provides support for women faculty of color (WFOC) and your teaching—which the scholarship of teaching and learning, teaching centers, and colleagues simply do not do. (Not a woman of color? See endnote.[1])

This book does so by focusing on your specific teaching and career needs, which are not the same as other faculty's. Though your teaching experience may well be ignored, silenced, dismissed, or treated as abnormal elsewhere, not here. Here, your teaching excellence is centered and will be celebrated. You can count on every evidence-based strategic action in this book to be tailored for you—as a woman of color and no one else. Period.

Our Goals on This Journey

As you step into the guts of the book, I hope you'll keep its three overarching goals in mind:

- To empower you to address common gender and race teaching challenges that WFOC face;
- To protect and champion your teaching through the institutional review process, thus reducing the stress and actual career threats you experience as WFOC; and
- To equip you to teach more authentically in a way that amplifies your gifts while making space for joy as a WFOC.

In working on these outcomes together, here's my commitment to you. I'm not going to pretend you have limitless time to deal with structural teaching problems that aren't even your fault, because I know you don't. Nor will I pretend all faculty are the same, because we're not. And we're going to stay away from confusing and vapid jargon, because we have enough of that.

Let's Talk about Trust

Because of the historical injustices and broken trust that litter the experiences of women faculty of color, I know that you cracking open this book is a big deal. You have a lot of good reasons to be skeptical, and I take your initial act of trust seriously. Hopefully, the 25 years and tens of thousands of hours of hands-on work I have give you the faith to read on. And we can build on that trust chapter by chapter.

Look . . . I could tell you that I'm a tenured full professor of sociology and that I earned my PhD in sociology and an MA in higher education at the University of Michigan with expertise in structural oppression, higher education, and methods/statistics. But what will probably give you the most reassurance is this:

I am a Black woman academic with lots of experience on the battlefield called an academic career for women faculty of color today. Severe lack of support? Check. Betrayals by the institution, big and small? Yep. Diverse statuses in the classroom, overloads, resistant students, surveilling colleagues, problematic teaching evaluations, you name it, I've seen it, heard it, and dealt with it for a plethora of women faculty of color. The roots of this book are personal and the lessons in it hard won, and sharing with you has been a long time coming. So thanks. Thanks in advance for the trust inherent in opening up this book.

Some Little-Known Facts and Corresponding Caveats

Now that you know you'll be centered in this book, let's get ourselves situated. The reality of life as a woman faculty of color is pretty stark. In fact, it can be downright devastating, and if you've gone through any of that, I stand with you in grief and acknowledgment.

With that, we aren't going to shy away from the truth in this book, because it's what's real and keeping the truth hidden is not going to serve us in the least. So here are some researched facts that you may not know exist:

- Women faculty of color are frequently assigned (1) heavier teaching loads, (2) more new course preparations, and (3) more service courses with larger enrollments. Fact.
- White students are more likely to undermine the authority of women faculty of color and two times more likely to inappropriately challenge these faculty when the course content is about race, gender, etc. Facts.
- Universities contribute to the demise of women faculty of color retention by using biased student evaluation scores and comments to deny their retention, tenure, and promotion. Fact.
- Women of color are severely underrepresented in full-time U.S. faculty at all ranks (essentially comprising less than 1–7 percent of faculty depending on the racial group.) Say it with me: Fact.

Even if you aren't shocked to read about these research-backed statements, and you're saying "Yep, that's my life," I hope laying them out cuts through any fogginess about what you've been trying to work through.

On the other hand, if reading this list stops you in your tracks, good. Good, because you seeing the threats clearly means we can get real about addressing them, together.

Now before you say, "Oh I should bring this to the attention of my teaching center, refer to the Scholarship of Teaching and Learning, or . . . share with some colleagues," in theory, yes, that is a logical step you might take. However, as deeply regrettable as it is, the reality right now is that these conventional resources have not been proven to support women faculty who look like you and me.

We will get into this more in each of the chapters to come, but consider these statements, which are also based in fact:

- The Scholarship of Teaching and Learning (SoTL) often ignores our teaching experiences with students, colleagues, and in institutional reviews.
- White and/or male colleagues and mentors often dismiss and demonize our teaching experiences as women faculty of color because they are different than theirs.
- Teaching centers offer advice that doesn't fit our positionality or social locations as women of color and therefore fail at supporting us though others regularly suggest these centers to us as a place for support.

Frankly, traditional sources of help often make our challenges worse, increasing threats to us and our careers. So yes. It's stark out there and tough to look at head-on. But it's why we're here, why this book exists, and why you're reading.

About You: A Brief Self-Assessment

Okay. Let's take a moment now and hear from you. What's real for you? Being compassionate about where you are is the name of the game, so take a few moments and identify where you are in each of the below statements. You might say to yourself "That sucks!" after each bullet. Simply find a writing instrument and answer "yes," "no," "somewhat," or another answer of your choice:

- I'm dedicated to great teaching and student learning but am beginning to feel exhausted and burnt out.
- I feel clueless about how to respond to problematic student interactions.
- I'm spending so much time on teaching there's no time left for research and writing.
- I feel ashamed of student evaluation scores and colleague reviews of my teaching.
- I find myself stealing time and attention away from loved ones to do course prep and grade.
- I'm worried about backlash against my teaching content, methods, or goals.
- I received or think I might get a negative retention, tenure, or promotion review due to my teaching load or reviews.

When you're done, take just a few minutes to look at the bigger picture. Do your answers take you aback, or are they all too familiar? Can you give yourself some validation for where you are today? Do that. There will be more validation, and of course suggestions and actions for each of these in the following pages. But do pause in this moment and give yourself some kind words of acknowledgment. I'm here for it.

There Is Light at the End of the Tunnel

We've given you some real talk here in this introduction and hopefully you feel seen, heard, and in the right place.

Now remember that vision for your campus life that we discussed earlier? The one where you can:

- ... birth a bounty of intellectual ideas [✔ without interference or distraction]
- ... be celebrated for your diverse ideas [✔ instead of punished as divisive or not scholarly]
- ... rightfully earn renewal, tenure, and promotion [✔ in lieu of teaching ruining your career]
- ... rest and be joyful [✔ versus being vigilant 24/7 due to structural threats to WFOC]

Your job now is to keep reading. That's all. That's all you need to concern yourself with. Read on.

If you'll do that one thing, here are a few words from women faculty of color who have worked with me that you, too, could be saying:

- "I am taking better care of myself and regularly engaging in my joy practices. I feel calmer. The dark cloud that was accompanying me everywhere has lifted. I feel more grounded."
- "I am developing my teaching portfolio and increasing the positive use of course evaluations in my review materials."
- "I feel empowered to learn how to be intentional and protect my career."

Take it from our sister academics from around the world whose words are above. There is light at the end of the tunnel. You can be unapologetically authentic in your teaching and succeed. I can't tell you how overjoyed I am as I hear from faculty, administrators, and teaching centers around the world, every single time a woman of color like you and me gets retained/tenured/promoted.

It's Your Turn: Chapter 1 Awaits

Dog-eared, worn-out cover. Notes on every other page. If not stolen from the library exactly, then passed along to others again and again. Consulted anytime you encounter teaching threats to your career. Laughter and welcome outrage in each chapter, all the way from cover to cover. That's what's ahead when you keep reading.

Here's to your joyful and empowered academic career.
I can't wait to see what you do next.

Chavella

HOW TO USE THIS BOOK

In case you haven't noticed yet, this isn't a regular ol' academic book. Nope. It's not a book you'll just "read."

To begin, read with a pencil in hand or a notepad close by. Make notes as you go from start to finish. The strategies layer and combine to provide the ultimate empowerment and career protection for your teaching, so it's almost certain you'll have insights and action steps to jot down.

Based on early reader feedback, it's very likely you won't refer to this book only once. As teaching issues arise, you will find it a source of ongoing solutions—including simple and quick actions to take. All this to say, empowering yourself and your career isn't a passive process, so get ready to act as you read this book!

You will find the following sections in each chapter:

- **Threat:** In this section, I describe a common teaching obstacle that stymies the well-being of women faculty of color. My goal is to ensure you can NAME the threat, SEE it, and know you're NOT alone. These are structural threats . . . not personal failings.
- **Strategic Action:** In this section, I guide you step-by-step through an evidence-based strategy to address the teaching threat so it doesn't tank your retention, tenure, and promotion reviews or teaching excellence. Bonus: These actions

require minimal time and energy since I know WFOC don't have extra of either to spare!
- **SoTL Minefield:** Here, I provide cautionary information and wave the red danger flag about how the Scholarship of Teaching and Learning (SoTL) contributes to the demise of and/or fails WFOC, their teaching, and careers. Knowing this information grounds and further empowers you.
- **Empowering Actions You Can Take This Week:** This is where you'll find micro actions you can take immediately to be more empowered—and I hope you will!

If you didn't know already, a heads-up that there are erroneous but widely popular narratives that label women of color's teaching as deficient. Although these narratives can beat us down, and although they presume something is wrong with us and our teaching, the evidence firmly points to the contrary. When that false narrative is particularly egregious or rampant, you'll also see this section in the chapter:

- **Excellence of WFOC's Teaching:** This section shares and allows you to revel in what the research demonstrates are the unique strengths and excellence in our teaching! I don't care how many times you read these sections, just get this in your bones, and use that evidence in your reviews.

And of course, each chapter includes a **Summary** for quick reference and review; this is where you'll find high-level takeaways.

Read, take notes, do some empowering actions, enact the strategies. Then continue to come back and do it again until you find yourself in a very different place from where you are now. Show up with an open mind and be willing to engage, and guess what? I'll be with you every step of the way with truth bombs, guidance, tough talk, encouragement, and sometimes even giggles. And you know what? If you get any of that from this book, I hope you will share it with others. We need all of us as empowered as possible in academe, end of story.

Bottom line? This book is like having a mentor in book form, available around the clock. And if that isn't enough . . . heck . . .

just reach out to me (empowered@effectivefaculty.org) if you get stuck.

Now let's get going so you can kiss teaching obstacles to your career bye-bye and say HELLO to the successful academic career you've earned and deserve.

Chapter 1

ESTABLISH THE HIGH GROUND

Learn how to make your teaching genius a fortress and get recognition for your efforts.

Gone are the days of feeling alone, wrong, or as if your teaching is being attacked from all sides and in all ways.

△ *Professor Mary Sanchez[1]—a Puerto Rican historian—is seen regularly escorted from her classroom by the police who are there to keep her safe from combative critics.*

After countless reports against her by her business school students, colleagues, and neighboring business owners, Korean American Dr. Lisa Lee has been denied tenure.

Assistant Professor Tanisha Jones is an African American STEM faculty member who gets death threats over email, leading to many of her talks being canceled by the powers-that-be. △

You may be wondering: What could these women of color faculty members have done to face or be on the receiving end of attacks like these, and a kaleidoscope of others?! Are they doing or saying something that's against the law? Perhaps they're failing at their job responsibilities and need to be fired? They must be doing something that warrants this kind of severe reaction, right?

The answer is heartbreaking, but true: Nope. Not even a little bit.

So what's going on, and what can be done about it—especially before it ends their academic careers? A lot! Stay with me while I lay it out so it's 100 percent clear.

Faculty members around the world who face attacks like those at the start of this chapter are women faculty of color who are just doing their jobs and doing them well. I'm guessing you can relate, and that you have many of your own stories. Well, from dozens of campus visits, I've witnessed it firsthand, and the latest research shows[2] you are simply teaching your scholarship and preparing students for the world, period, full stop. Right? You're not breaking any laws, or being derelict in your teaching work. You are actually EXCEEDING your teaching responsibilities. So what's going on with the threats and attacks from left to right, and top to bottom, to your teaching (and retention, tenure, and promotion)? Let's talk about it. Let's talk about all of it.

Excellence of WFOC's Teaching:
Unique Pedagogy, Goals, and Benefits

Women faculty of color: Your teaching is awesome. That's worth saying outright with emphasis! Of course, we don't all teach the same way. But there *are* some identifiable patterns, if you will, in how we teach that are unique to us as women faculty of color. We'll delve further into each pattern in the pages to come, but for right now, I want to start with an overview. The goal here is to reveal the types of teaching choices women faculty of color generally make so you can locate yourself within these patterns, feel affirmed, and gain confidence that you're not alone in how you teach. In other words, it is A-okay to teach the way you do. As you'll see . . . our teaching choices are MORE than okay. The choices we make are the very definition of excellence in teaching according to the scholarship of teaching and learning.

The three main patterns of excellence that are noticeable and distinctive in your teaching approach as a woman faculty of color are as follows.

#1 Excellence via Innovative and Transformative Pedagogy

Women faculty of color, guess what? The report card is in and the data show your use of innovative and transformative pedagogy is off-the-charts!

Research shows that we are innovative teachers.[3] For example, we are more likely than white and male faculty to use transformative pedagogical techniques known empirically to improve learning.[4] In addition, we are more likely than our privileged-status peers to use pedagogy that requires our students' active participation in their learning.[5] We teach by engaging our students to collaborate with us and their peers.[6] This begs the question, "Why doesn't every faculty member use these pedagogies?" Never mind, they don't,[7] and that's what makes this worth you noticing. Translation: You can be proud as heck of your pedagogy.

#2 Excellence via Teaching Goals That Go beyond the Status Quo

Your teaching goals are more than just facts and numbers. Women faculty of color—that's you—your awesome teaching also aims for deep learning and whole-student development!

Women faculty of color, did you know you tend to teach the whole student instead of providing only content knowledge? Just know that, for us, teaching is not an exercise to deposit knowledge into a passive vessel. No, you focus on higher-order cognitive learning in place of surface learning;[8] you aim to increase the affective, emotional, moral, and civic development of students[9] and even teach students the skills to understand, and contribute to, the wider world.[10] Women faculty of color also frequently teach students to question "objectivity" and to critically examine new information.[11] We even go so far as to help students recognize and question oppression in their daily lives.[12] And guess what? These unique teaching goals of yours—they supercharge student learning empowering them with a noticeably different level of integration. Think of what you do as a whole student learning, and be proud as heck of that, too.

#3 Excellence via Benefits to Your Campus and Society as a Whole

Women faculty of color, your extra contributions are thoroughly documented. Big props! Your efforts result in documented benefits to your campus and society, on top of supporting students.

Please have confidence in these facts: Women faculty of color dedicate more time attending to, advising, and mentoring students.[13] And of course, we include more activities and assignments connected to diversity and the real-world[14] infusing our classroom with the lived experiences that increase student engagement and a sense of belonging.[15] These teaching efforts of ours are consistently linked to not only student learning, but also to campus benefits like student persistence, and even the retention of students.[16] That's right, that's all you. The whole student development we do via our teaching goals? While they benefit individual students, they also benefit society by increasing civic, economic, and health outcomes—just to name a few. That's right, you go beyond lecture and book learning and help fulfill your institution's broadest vision and mission—creating good citizens of the world. Just wow! In short, the teaching you authentically employ is of great benefit to campuses and society[17] and a direct reflection of your excellence. Isn't it time you owned it?

Excellence Is as Excellence Does

You don't have to recognize yourself in the specific teaching examples above to accept this fact: Women faculty of color's teaching pedagogies, goals, and benefits to society and campus are excellent.

Whatever department you're in, whatever your specific teaching details, whatever courses you're balancing this academic term, and whichever type of institution you inhabit, women faculty of color, it's time to internalize this truth: Your teaching is amazing! Which is what makes the reality of what happened to Drs. Mary, Tanisha, and Lisa all the more unfortunate.

But what about you? Have you encountered the most common narrative about women of color's teaching? That something is wrong with it and it must be fixed?[18] I bet you'd like to know that the research on our teaching does not bear this narrative out. In fact, research says the exact opposite about our teaching quality: It says it's awesome and adds tremendous value. But instead of winning awards and having our teaching highlighted and emulated—we get challenged and resisted like the women faculty of color in the opening of this chapter.

Threat:

Are They with Us or Against Us? Resistance to Women Faculty of Color's Excellent Teaching

In light of the research, it's clear women of color should be winning awards for their teaching excellence. We're creating results for students, overdelivering on expectations relative to our peers, and helping institutions fulfill their bigger mandates, including increased student persistence, retention, and bettering societal outcomes. Yet rather than being valued, our teaching is instead being attacked and resisted[19] and causing failed renewal, tenure, and promotion attempts. It's true that the attacks aren't always as conspicuous or as violent as the ones we generally hear about; or exactly like the threats to our physical safety like the examples I gave earlier. These acute cases get media attention, but what's more common is insidious on a daily level—attacks on our teaching in the form of ongoing day-by-day, hour-by-hour, meeting-by-meeting resistance, from both students and colleagues. It's important for you to understand the simple and pervasive existence of resistance to what you do every day inside your classroom that ultimately tanks your career reviews.

> "Alright then, Chavella, I hear you. There's systemic resistance to my teaching and it's tough to be clear who's with me and who's against me. I get that. I feel it, too. It's heavy! But what I want to know is what does the scholarly research on resistance say, actually? And why should I care about that?"

I get asked this a lot, and I'm always so glad because it gives me hope that you're ready to empower yourself and have a different experience in your classrooms and reviews. Here's just a handful of bullets you can refer to as needed to (1) know you aren't alone—this is a systemic issue for women faculty of color, (2) equip you with facts to use in intentional conversations with peers to shape the narrative of your experiences, and (3) explicitly cite in your review materials as an offense or defense for resistance:

- *Women scholars of color commonly experience white male student attacks for what they teach and how they teach.* My study on raced and gendered classroom[20] experiences found that these experiences are neither anecdotal nor isolated.
- *White male colleagues have been documented behaving aggressively toward women of color's transformative teaching methods.*[21] These teaching methods seem to pose a threat

to the more traditional approach of teaching primarily through lectures. This resistance is one of the most common themes I hear from being on campus—the constant and intense pressure from white colleagues, chairs, and deans to revert to lecture-only teaching.
- *White students have been found to disproportionately challenge the authority of women faculty of color.*[22] And they are twice as likely to aggressively question them when being taught about social justice issues.[23]
- *When WFOC teach topics like race, white colleagues antagonistically label this as marginal and illegitimate knowledge.*[24] Imagine being one of my women of color clients who were told by administrators to abandon race scholarship and teach the white male "classics" instead. It's a head scratcher, right?! Don't worry, we'll get into how you can handle that kind of conundrum in the pages to come.
- *Women of color academics face virulent outrage and threats to their safety—from those outside the academy—for teaching scholarship on social inequality, or topics that challenge the status quo.*[25] It has become common for me to hear from women of color that they've been doxxed by extremists—people who goad the public into harassing, threatening, and harming them and their families—with little institutional help.

Well, there it is in black and white, the facts from the literature in a list of undeniable bullets. You're welcome! Because perhaps you've sensed resistance to your teaching before, but couldn't quite put your finger on it, right? Now you know for sure. Like trying to paddle a boat against the current underneath you, or walking up the down escalator, even though you're putting forth energy, you're not imagining things if you feel you're not getting where you should.

Even women of color who teach relatively traditionally will say to me:

"I'm doing all the normal things everyone else is doing. I don't understand what I'm doing wrong? No matter what I do there is resistance."

Here is what I hope will help with this realization: What you're experiencing is real, and the resistance may be to your simple existence! If this sounds confronting, it is, because the attacks are rooted in your marginalized race and gender statuses. In a way, it's not personal to you as an individual because no matter your teaching choices, they will be viewed as illegitimate by students and colleagues. To them, their gendered racist reactions and resistance are natural and well-founded.

Okay, let's take a moment to let this sink in. In my experience, sometimes naming the resistance as real is a relief. It's a 'Yes!' moment akin to the light going on after you've been fumbling in the dark. Other times, this new awareness of resistance in your life can feel like a gut punch, and take the wind out of your sails. Or, you may feel something totally different in this moment. Whatever you're experiencing, it's okay to take a moment and process. When you're ready, let's move on.

Here's How Their Resistance Corrodes Your Academic Future

People always say "Oh, academic success is all about scholarly productivity." Well, duh, yeah, it is. But how can you focus on that when you're having to manage a battlefield of resistance to your teaching on the daily? Here's the deal. Your awareness of this resistance (while freeing and relieving) isn't enough. You have to ACT to defang and ultimately curtail the attacks on your teaching. This is because these attacks can have significant negative consequences for you and your career:

- *Lowered research productivity.*[26] It takes extra time and energy for you to manage the hostile students in your classroom, colleague opposition, and public outcries to your teaching. This then reduces the finite time, mental and emotional energy you have to produce research, publications, and grants. And thus, this results in less of this productivity currency that's needed for a successful renewal, promotion, or tenure review.

- *Powerful pressure and decries from outside the academy to fire or otherwise punish you.* When influences outside the academy generate tsunamis of negative media attention for universities and encourage donors to pull financial support in efforts to silence women faculty of color's classroom content.[27] Universities frequently cave to this pressure to remove WFOC by rescinding their hire offers, firing them or failing their retention, tenure, or promotion bids.
- *Negative student evaluations and colleague observations.* Getting negative feedback is one thing, but when your institution legitimizes it, and uses it to deny your retention, promotion, or tenure, we're talking about a level of consequence to your career that can be catastrophic. Whether a result of race and gender biases[28] or something else, this is not something to shrug off, thinking it will go away, or bury your head in the sand about. Not this kind of outcome, not on my watch, nope.
- *Forced exits from the institution.* Constant battles with students, colleagues, and the public resisting *your* classroom authority, pedagogy, and content is incredibly taxing.[29] In fact, it can lead to burnout and serious mental and physical health consequences. When institutions don't guard women faculty of color from undue resistance[30] they can be forced to leave. And of course that forced exit is the opposite of retention, to say the least.

In short, your retention, tenure, and promotion will continue to be at risk when resistance is left unchecked. You didn't work hard for your career to let potholes on the teaching road wreck it, so we're going to go into detail about all of this.

Awareness Opens the Door to Empowerment and Action

I hope this information, drawn directly from current scholarly literature, brings home in vivid terms what resistance to your teaching—and its negative outcomes—looks like to, and for, us. The bullets above represent the environment and daily teaching experiences of faculty who look like us. It's real, has destructive consequences for your academic career, and it's not going away anytime soon. However, the good news is you can change how you equip yourself to respond. You can put yourself in the driver's seat of how you protect yourself and your career with daily actions. Doing that is how you'll find a path to thrive.

Let's Learn from Our Sisters

Suffice to say, the reason I'm so over-the-top committed to empowering you in your academic career—and the entire reason this book exists—is because of stories like this, woman faculty of color:

Assistant Professor Karla Brown,[31] in a public letter, described unchecked hostilities as the reason she left her institution. I'll say it differently: The consequences of student and faculty hostility led to her leaving her institution—and all she had invested there—because things got just that bad. And the institution did nothing to combat that hostility.

What Dr. Brown says is what's happening to all of us, one day at a time:

> "There are not enough white faculty and administrators willing to publicly teach white students how to hold themselves accountable for their racist behavior in the classroom. This unpaid emotional labor is often left to Black and Brown faculty who recognize it, feel it, and (all alone) are left to call it out.
>
> It is exhausting work and doesn't win us any favors with colleagues and administrators."

Look, this is real talk. Quite simply—I don't want this to happen to you. I don't want it to happen to anyone. I want it to happen the LEAST to women faculty of color—some of the most valuable players on campus. Let's learn from our sisters and forge a different path. You ready?

Strategic Action:

It's Time to Protect Your Career and Empower Yourself. Here's How . . .

The Women Faculty of Color's Best Friend: A Succinct and Transparent Keystone Statement

What should be clear at this point is that you have to both protect your academic career and empower yourself! You *have* to protect yourself from these challenges so that you can maintain the authentic teaching that you're doing and earn retention/tenure/promotion. After all, the goal is for you to teach authentically and thrive in academe. To do so as a woman of color, you have to protect yourself including your career.

As we progress through this book, you'll learn that while I'm a fan of game-changing ideas, I will equally insist on practical, actionable takeaways, and here's our first one. You must have a succinct, transparent, and strategic statement that will provide a force field around your teaching and career. There are many additional protective and empowering strategies in the book, but this one is the center of it all. It is your keystone.

Keystone:

> "a central stone at the summit of an arch, locking the whole together."
>
> "the central principle or part of a policy, system, etc., on which all else depends."
>
> Oxford University Press Dictionary, n.d.[32]

With your strategic statement about teaching in place as your personal keystone, you will have a way to protect and empower yourself in a catch-all manner. This way—if you don't have the time or energy right now to look at the other strategies in this book, you'll at least have this important strategy in place. How will we achieve that? We're going to break it down right here, right now, so you can start deploying it this week. All you have to do is follow along with your ideas as we go.

The key point about the succinct and transparent statement for women faculty of color is this: This statement isn't meant to share useless philosophical and intellectual ideas about teaching. It is a purposeful statement with intentionality about your career protection and empowerment. This statement is your protection from the dark arts. It is not an exercise only about bettering teaching. For us, it's an exercise about being strategic as all get out in the face of resistance. And once crafted as I urge, this statement cannot only be in your head. It must be in black and white on your syllabus, and in your conversations with colleagues and students. It most definitely needs to be in your teaching review materials.

We'll talk in a couple of pages about why having a succinct and transparent teaching statement is so crucial to your empowerment in the face of challenges. Right now, let's focus on how exactly you will craft yours.

With that in mind—an effective KEYSTONE teaching (philosophy) statement is made up of three components:[33]

> *Component #1: What do you think about teaching? What are your ideas about teaching?*
>
> *Component #2: What do you want students to get out of your courses?*
>
> *Component #3: How do you move students toward what you want them to get?*

If these three components are present, you have yourself a keystone statement. If not, you don't.

We're going to take these one by one in a moment, but here's where the rubber meets the road. In my many conversations with faculty about teaching (philosophy) statements, the issues are glaring. Teaching philosophy statements are either completely overlooked or underdone. People either admit they don't know how to write a teaching philosophy at all, they feel insecure about the one they've written, or the ones who feel confident about their teaching philosophy have actually produced one that isn't great (or even good!). They may have a statement of teaching philosophy, but it is all fluff and no stuff. A bunch of words strung together with little to no substance.

What we want to create for you is a teaching (philosophy) statement that's neither overlooked or underdone—one that is just right to protect your teaching and career.

After all, given the institutional challenges we face, we don't have the luxury of a teaching philosophy statement that's mediocre, unintentional, or non-strategic. Are there a zillion things you could add in and address in your statement of teaching philosophy? Yes, sure. Do you have the time and energy to do and deal with all of that? No. Is all of that stuff necessary for our purposes? Also, no.

So let's aim for the just-right version right now, are you with me? Alright, let's get started.

Component #1: What Are Your Thoughts about Teaching (i.e., Your Overarching Beliefs about Teaching)?

This may sound like it is and should be complicated but it doesn't require fancy pants ways to describe what you think about teaching. Too often this question alone is what stumps folks, and we're not going to let that happen here. So take a moment and ask yourself the version of this question that's easiest for you:

What are your thoughts about teaching?
What core beliefs do you have about teaching?
What would you say is important about teaching?

As you answer, just allow your thoughts to flow. You can't get this wrong and we're just getting you warmed up. What big picture answers come to mind? A high level, broad description of your view of teaching is what we're ultimately going for.

> **Here are some examples:**
> - Your view is that teaching is an act that liberates students. Or,
> - You teach so that students develop an appreciation of history. Or,
> - Your teaching ensures students acquire the necessary knowledge to get to the next course level.

As you can see, component #1, your thoughts about teaching, is a concise way to represent your broad ideas about teaching.

Component #2: What Do You Want Students to Get Out of Your Courses (i.e., Your Teaching Goals)?

In this second part of your keystone statement, you get to describe in broad terms what you want students to gain from your teaching—as it relates to your ideas about teaching. That is, your teaching goals are an elaboration of your overarching ideas about teaching. They reflect an overarching view of what you want students to learn—the outcomes you want for them (but without getting into the weeds and details).

Let's take our previous examples and elaborate so you can see the connection between the first two components, and as we go along, notice any ideas that come up about what your teaching goals are.

Example #1:

Point of view on teaching (component #1):

Teaching is an act that liberates students ...

Broad-stroke teaching goal (component #2):

... so that they can become the best and empowered version of themselves.

Broad-stroke teaching goal (component #2) translated into SoTL learning goals:

This broad teaching goal results in students' social, moral, and emotional development; social mobility; and acquiring employer-valued knowledge and skills.

Example #2:

Point of view on teaching (component #1):

I teach so that students develop an appreciation of history and better understand the world.

Broad-stroke teaching goal #1 (component #2):

With this understanding, they can then better understand and participate in the world.

Broad-stroke teaching goal #1 (component #2) translated into SoTL learning goals:

This broad teaching goal results in students developing as active citizens, improving their critical thinking, and increasing political participation/voting, etc.

Broad-stroke teaching goal #2 (component #2):

As a result, they welcome diverse perspectives and can communicate across differences.

Broad-stroke teaching goal #2 (component #2) translated into SoTL learning goals:

This broad teaching goal provides students with communication skills across different cultures, higher order cognitive skills, and an understanding of diverse perspectives.

Example #3:

Point of view on teaching (component #1):

It's important to me that my teaching ensures students acquire the necessary knowledge to get to the next course level.

> Broad-stroke teaching goal (component #2):
>
> *My goal is that students successfully complete their education.*
>
> Broad-stroke teaching goal (component #2) translated into SoTL learning goals:
>
> *The teaching goal here ensures students acquire content knowledge, skills, competencies, and financial stability and mobility.*

You see through these three examples that there is a wide variety of views and goals, each unique to the individual woman faculty of color. Yours will sound uniquely yours as well.

After identifying your broad idealistic teaching goal, you also have to bring it home with the official language of student goals as I've done in the "translations into SoTL" above. This keeps you from being eaten alive by detractors' claims of your goals as irrelevant or illegitimate. If you see SoTL language in the examples and think: "Who knew that's what SoTL calls my goal?" or "Wow, that's exactly what I do!"—add it to your keystone statement. If not, don't worry about the specific jargony learning goals part. I've got you as we'll talk about that more later in the book where I'll provide you with a ton more examples of learning goals that are sure to cover exactly what's in your teaching.

To recap, your teaching goals are the broad outcomes you hope your teaching produces in students. Remember, you're going to use these components to build a succinct and transparent teaching statement which you will lean on in multiple places to fortify your teaching defenses—especially in reviews.

And now onto the final component before we start putting your version of your statement together. You're getting there!

Component #3: How Do You Move Students toward Your Teaching Goals (i.e., Your Teaching Strategies)?

The final component in your succinct and transparent statement is the most tangible and practical one: What do you do to move students toward your teaching goals? What are the methods you use to get students where you want them to go? These are your "teaching strategies"—the way in which you help students gain your desired outcomes.

Once you think about it, this component is pretty straightforward.

> **Here are some examples of this component:**
>
> Do you use . . .
>
> Interactive lectures? Discussions? Projects? Community engagement? Role plays? And so on.

Your teaching strategies are the ways you help students reach the teaching goals you've established for your course. When you think about it—what are some of the teaching strategies you currently use to get students where you want them to go? Write those down.

The Final Product: a Succinct and Transparent KEYSTONE Teaching Statement

And ta-da, using the three components above, here's an example that would be shared on a syllabus, in conversations with students and colleagues, and in teaching review materials.

> I teach so that students develop an appreciation of history so they can better understand (i.e., cognitive skill, critical thinking) and participate in the world (i.e., political participation, active citizenship). That appreciation requires them

> to learn diverse perspectives in history (i.e., knowledge acquisition) and develop the ability to communicate across those differences (i.e., skill development). To move students toward these learning goals they need to fully engage in the course ideas instead of passively consuming them. As such my teaching includes active learning strategies such as interactive lectures, discussions, role plays, etc.

And there you have it. Hopefully you see that this succinct KEYSTONE teaching philosophy statement can be completed by collecting and massaging your ideas about the three component questions: What are your thoughts about teaching? What do you want students to get out of your courses? How do you move students toward these wants?

Guess what? You now know the three steps to creating the woman faculty of color's best friend: An intentional and strategic statement of your teaching philosophy, what I call your keystone. This keystone can—and will—fundamentally improve your daily academic experience and preparation for retention, tenure, and promotion reviews. The only thing missing is implementation.

How and Why This Strategy Empowers You to Advocate for Yourself

Congratulations! Now that you're clear on how to draft your own unique KEYSTONE teaching philosophy statement, you may wonder why I'm so passionate about this as a way to protect your teaching from attacks and review denials.

On the surface, I'm suggesting it because it's an evidence-based teaching practice that supports teaching excellence and student learning.[34] The facts are that:

- Those who assemble these statements have intentional and better-planned teaching, which increases student learning.
- Writing a teaching philosophy statement requires faculty to self-reflect on their teaching—which improves teaching leading to more student learning.

- The practice of sharing your teaching philosophy statement with students increases transparency about learning that boosts their academic outcomes.

You can and should discuss all of these facts as evidence of your teaching effectiveness with colleagues and in your reviews.

On a deeper level, a statement of teaching philosophy protects you and the teaching choices you're making from the resistance you face from colleagues, students, and the public. This is because it makes it clear and transparent that your teaching is credible. Since it communicates your ideas about teaching and learning, how you teach, and why, the strategy of having a teaching statement makes it crystal clear that you have a cohesive plan for your teaching, its goals, and how students will learn. You're not making haphazard choices. You have intentional pieces that fit together. Get it? It's harder to attack your teaching (especially in reviews) when it's presented as a cohesive whole and part of the plan. And to make this plain, dominant status faculty should also have transparency about their teaching statement. Regrettably, they usually don't.

Take a moment to close your eyes and imagine this: A group of women warriors of color. At first, they're scattered across a large open space. Fierce individuals able to defend themselves. And then suddenly, you see them standing shoulder to shoulder holding their shields up—together—in a tight circle formation. In which formation do they appear more vulnerable? Which one provides them protection on all sides?

Your teaching philosophy statement provides this same perimeter or all-around defense for your teaching and reviews. Your individual teaching choices—topics, assignments, readings, learning goals, practices—are exemplars of teaching excellence. Yet, when viewed separately and independently of each other, they can be perceived by students, colleagues, and reviewers as vulnerable and open to attack—just like a lone warrior. A succinct and transparent teaching statement connects your teaching choices into a formation together to provide more security and protection.

So instead of presenting discrete choices such as "I decided to assign this reading" or "I decided to have this type of assignment" which may seem haphazard or debatable to others and thus open to resistance, choose to put forward your teaching as a cohesive whole. All the discrete choices combine to form a circle. "My teaching philosophy is _____." By doing this, your teaching goes from debatable to defendable, from haphazard to cohesive, from being attacked, to being more recognized and even—it can happen—emulated. And not only that—your life as a woman of color academic has the opportunity to become much more rewarding (e.g., tenure) and joyful—what you signed up for when you decided on this career path in the first place!

The strategic KEYSTONE teaching philosophy statement isn't a magic pill, but close. If you're discovering anything about me in these pages so far, you know that I'm never going to lead you down a false rosy path. We keep it real here. So here's the real talk. All of the above doesn't mean that folks aren't going to challenge your teaching ever again. If only! No, systemic issues don't come down quite that easily. However, having this transparent way of talking about your teaching that's grounded in the SoTL literature is going to reveal attacks as groundless, if not downright foolish, and attackers as simply wrong. Connect your teaching choices to intentional course design, make plain that you know that everyone should be doing this, clearly communicate that to people, and, well, your teaching experiences and reviews will be a whole lot better.

Bonus Strategic Action:
And Then, There's Academic Freedom

Just one more thing. The SoTL helps you defend your teaching against attacks, and that's a good thing. In addition though, you have another pillar of empowerment available to you and that is academic freedom. (Current context posing explicit threats to academic freedom? Read this endnote.[35])

If you're thinking "how the heck does academic freedom help me here?" I got you. It's actually a very strong backstop for you. Let's start with this explanation of academic freedom:

32 CHAPTER 1

> the freedom to teach includes the right of the faculty to select the materials, determine the approach to the subject, make the assignments, and assess student academic performance in teaching activities for which faculty members are individually responsible. Faculty members are entitled to freedom in the classroom in discussing their subject . . . As long as the material stimulates debate and learning that is germane to the subject matter, it is protected by freedom in the classroom.[36]

Boom.

Let this be a reminder to us all, including any naysayers or challengers, anyone trying to challenge what you're doing in the classroom—so long as the teaching stimulates learning germane to the subject matter—there are no grounds for attack. Someone's trying to say that your teaching philosophy is wrong? That your classroom strategies are too much, or too little? What grounds do they have to say that, so long as learning is happening? None. Nope. Uh uh. Plain and simple. In summary, frame your teaching with a teaching philosophy statement in discussions and reviews, and you'll be less open to attack. You're organized and have a plan. If you're ever questioned about it, here are the strategic actions. I encourage you to question back: Is the questioner's teaching philosophy up for debate? Are there consequences to them for their teaching choices—such as potentially losing their position? Is there surveillance about their teaching philosophy? Again, there shouldn't be any of this, not for the questioner, not for you, not for any woman faculty of color, so those questioners can back off. Make the case plain and quote the protections of academic freedom as needed in your conversations and your review materials.

SoTL Minefield:

Assumptions about Power (i.e., the Force Field)

Okay, we're covering a lot of ground, and I want to commend you for the sheer guts and commitment it takes for you to contend with all of this. I hope the steps I share with you make things doable one step at a time. My promise in this book is to give you a clear view into how to become the best, most empowered version of you. To do that, I never want you to be caught off guard, so there's something we have to come to terms with. There's much strength to be derived from the research in the SoTL—the teaching philosophy statement is one of them—but it has its limits. One of SoTL's limits is the way it makes assumptions about power.

The SoTL rarely talks about the structural privilege and power required to teach effectively. By not talking about either openly, it makes all sorts of assumptions about the privilege, power, and *authority* that faculty have in their teaching choices and philosophy. To decide what students will do, how they'll do it, and to facilitate and require those things requires power. The SoTL just assumes that the teaching philosophy and other teaching choices of women faculty of color will be accepted and protected. And that is NOT the case. When white or male faculty come into the classroom with more assumed inherent power than we do, SoTL has to acknowledge that inequity, or they miss the boat.

Would it surprise you if I say the power and privilege afforded to faculty with dominant statuses (e.g., white male faculty) pretty much does the heavy lifting of teaching authority in the classroom? That those dominant statuses grant them great ease and that academic freedom—for them—comes naturally with that? It doesn't matter if they have a vague, ineffective, or nonexistent teaching philosophy. It doesn't matter if they have nontraditional or ineffective teaching practices because they wear academic freedom and the authority to uphold their teaching choices in their skin.

Here's what I mean by in their skin—a lot of your privileged faculty colleagues don't understand that teaching requires that students recognize faculty authority. Instead they criticize efforts to establish teaching authority—a common example is white male professors who deride women of color faculty who require students to call them Doctor. Teaching authority[37] doesn't mean authoritative; classroom or teaching authority means that you have the right and duty to choose the learning material and activities required in the classroom. And the right and duty to shape the classroom environment so it's conducive to learning—things like setting boundaries.

Here's an exercise: Notice who has a built-in force field of authority, expertise, skill, and academic freedom to protect their teaching. Now, who doesn't have that built-in and has to work for it—sometimes ongoingly, sometimes ceaselessly?

A New Framework: Your Empowered Force Field

In order for you to thrive, you need a new framework and actionable steps to put that framework into place. The easiest way to think about privileged faculty and what's happening for them is to imagine a force field. The force field is students', colleagues', and outsiders' assumption and acceptance of privileged faculty's authority, expertise, and skill. This force field is like a fence that provides a protected space within. In the fenced-in space, privileged faculty can reliably and effectively teach. They don't have to worry about what's outside the fence, nor what's trying to get over or through the fence. They can just focus on teaching—get creative with assignment ideas, facilitate lively student discussions, connect real-world examples to the scholarship they are teaching, and even just relax and be themselves.

This force field is important to notice. It exists because all manner of people—students, colleagues, and people outside the academy—assume and readily accept the authority, expert status, and competency of privileged faculty. The force field is created because the status quo says privileged faculty are great, and nobody questions that. It is the default.

Here's the thing—faculty with privileged statuses don't even know the force field is there protecting them. They just experience the safety and space to get their teaching work done unfettered and undisturbed. The authority, expertise, and skill attached to their dominant statuses make this possible. And because it's their default, they assume most everybody else has the same experience.

In marked contrast, women of color faculty know the force field is there, and we know the one around us is different from the force fields of our white colleagues. Rather than healthy and robust, the force field around us is erratic, and tends to malfunction. Sometimes it works—our authority, expertise, and skills are given credit, and protect us from any naysayers. At other times, the force field fails. People unjustifiably question us, challenge our work, report, and sabotage us. As a result, our classroom is not a space of safety for us. Have you seen the famous dinosaur movie where the velociraptors are testing for weaknesses in the electric fence in a methodical and coordinated way? Colleagues, students, and powerful others can be like those velociraptors sometimes, testing our force field for weaknesses, looking for a way to get to us.

By taking into practice the strategies in this book, including the keystone statement in this chapter, you create a stronger empowered force field for yourself. As you keep reading, you will discover more ways to empower yourself as the legitimate convener of the classroom and boost your teaching authority. Although a well-functioning force field hasn't been gifted to us, we can—and must, if we want to thrive—engage in the strategies through the rest of this book to strengthen it ourselves.

Summary

Job well done completing this chapter that provides the strategy for your empowered foundation! Where the SoTL helps us, we use it and apply it by putting a keystone teaching statement in place, stat. And where the SoTL has holes, and mischaracterizes our authority, we take note. And we look for other sources of expertise, know-how, and allyship in order to take action anyway. This is how you'll establish the higher ground to protect your teaching and career.

As you plan your keystone statement and develop your empowered force field, keep these key ideas from this chapter in mind:

- Your teaching employs innovative and effective pedagogy focused on extraordinary student learning outcomes. It is beneficial to everyone, even the institution and society.
  In other words, WFOC teaching is awesome.

- Despite documented excellence, WFOC's teaching gets attacked leading to negative consequences to their career and more.
- You must use a strategic KEYSTONE statement to empower yourself. With it, you can more readily advocate for your teaching choices, student learning, and career. This strategic succinct and transparent teaching philosophy statement is the mother of all protective strategies—think of it as the keystone to your empowerment.
- The SoTL and academic freedom allow you to teach as you choose and see fit.
- The SoTL is helpful, but has holes. It should protect you and your teaching, but it doesn't do so fully. It overlooks the reality of structural power inequities in your and other WFOC's teaching experiences.
- Your teaching as a WFOC can't be just about student learning but must also put you in a position to be renewed, tenured, and promoted despite teaching inequities.
- While WFOC's teaching continues to be attacked, there are practical, doable strategies available to create an empowered force field around yourself and your career. I share some of those strategies in the rest of this book.

Empowering Actions You Can Take This Week

Which of these actions can you take this week? Studies show that reading a book can have the most impact when you take even the smallest action as soon as possible. I'm biased, but I'd like this book to take up more than space between your ears. I'd like the ideas to filter through your head and heart and take up space as you put your strategic actions out into the world!

1. Consider the fact that research backs up women faculty of color's teaching as exceptional. What feels different now that you know this? Who do you know who you can share this with?

2. Start working on your keystone teaching philosophy statement by taking 10 minutes to brainstorm answers to the question "What type of teacher am I?" There are no right or wrong answers, so don't overthink it.
3. Reach out to me at empowered@effectivefaculty.org if your university isn't standing up for your teaching choices as they SHOULD be, given the SoTL and academic freedom.
4. This week, before heading out in the morning, and perhaps also at night before you fall asleep, try to visualize an empowered force field of protection around you. Imagine yourself walking into class and submitting your teaching review materials protected in that way, knowing that your keystone statement has got your back.

What additional support, resources, or strategies would help you be more empowered in using your keystone statement in your reviews? What help could you use? There are many resources available, so don't hesitate to look for them. My email is available and is just one of those resources, too: empowered@effectivefaculty.org.

Now, read on to the next chapter to make sure all of your fantastic teaching labor counts toward retention/tenure/promotion instead of leaving you burnt out without anything tangible to show for it.

Chapter 2

ANCHOR TO STRONG POINTS

Gain crystal clarity about your teaching labor and don't let your generosity continue to go unnoticed.

Reap well-deserved benefits from this labor that steals time from writing/research/grants.

And at the same time, banish accusations of "bias" or "an agenda."

△ We all know her. In fact, you might know her as you. Whether that's you as you are today, or maybe a younger, more naive version of you. Who am I talking about? That woman of color who sits on every committee as the diversity person. Who's asked (or coerced) to spearhead every new diversity initiative, among others. The woman faculty who goes beyond the call of duty to serve students, including students of color outside the classroom, without being asked.

Inside the classroom, she's giving full out for all of these same students, too. Sometimes she does this work because it's her calling. Sometimes it's because she's been guilted or pressured to participate as the "only" woman in her department. Sound familiar? She wears her game face every day, saying yes to all manner of things, even when giving so much extra comes at her expense.

But it gets worse. Despite this unflagging extra effort on the part of this woman of color . . . you guessed it. The university delivers a crushing blow. It's a "no" to her tenure application. It's an entirely inexplicable "no" after almost a decade of grad school preparation and commitment to the pre-tenure track for five to seven years, a "no" that kills her academic career, and her financial livelihood. The next thing you know, this major contributor and beautiful soul is gone from the university. △

Threat:
The Insidiousness of Invisible Teaching Labor for Women Faculty of Color

To make this crystal clear, the above example shows how women faculty of color are required[1] to give, give, and give to the university—and then get discarded by it, after their labor has been greedily and shamelessly consumed.[2]

This "demand, use, and discard" or "DUD" phenomenon is not a one-off; it's a pattern embedded into institutions and a systemic phenomenon that disproportionately affects us:

> While seeking tenure and promotion, Black faculty and staff members are often asked to carry greater service burdens than their white colleagues. A 2019 study found that

women and faculty members of color take on a disproportionate amount of the "invisible" work in academia, such as serving on committees, mentoring and advising students, overseeing student organizations, and other community-based service. This service is subsequently devalued during tenure and promotional reviews.[3]

As if this isn't bad enough, let's kick it up a notch. The term "invisible labor" has become commonly understood to indicate the tangible work that falls through the cracks and goes unacknowledged in the dominant narrative. An example in the non-academic realm would be all of the labor that women might do. Laundry, making appointments for family, and even taking care of the mail. While the growing use of the term is a good thing, in the academy, the phrase "invisible labor" is almost exclusively used to refer to the labor like mentoring, advising, and community involvement that goes unacknowledged when diverse faculty perform this service which falls outside of traditional service like committee work, leadership roles, etc. Fabulous that this layer of invisible labor is being recognized, but this usage of the term falls short.

Super-Invisible Labor: In the Classroom

Here when I refer to invisible labor, I'm not talking about service labor. I'm focused instead on the trickier, more treacherous waters of invisible labor specific to your teaching and classroom labor. I make the case that these efforts are even more invisible than other contributions women of color faculty make, and point to why this is important. For now, suffice to say that in addition to the overload of labor in traditional service activities, teaching is its own separate and additional invisible labor category for women faculty of color. This invisible labor embedded in our teaching goes well beyond the greater time we spend on teaching in comparison to our white and male colleagues.[4]

Let's call this particular type of labor "super-invisible labor." If you think our regular service labor gets overlooked, then the added service we provide through our teaching is like the deep cover hard-to-see labor that doesn't even get looked for, so of course you don't get any "credit" for it. Certainly, it takes up additional time in our schedules, but *what* we do in our classrooms is actually perfectly aligned with the SoTL. Our teaching is excellent while everyone else's teaching is common (but not best) practice. Our invisible labor is serving big-picture university goals about teaching excellence, and yet is taken for granted or sucked up for university gain. Paying the price for doing this super-invisible labor without credit is becoming a familiar refrain, isn't it? Well, I hope it stops here, because that is the goal of this chapter: For you to embrace and stand strong in the credit due to you for this contribution to your university.

No more super-invisible labor for free!! Together, we're going to make certain you claim that teaching labor as tenure currency!

Claim Your Tenure Credit

Okay, wait just a second. I hear some voices. These are in my head, but they're there because I've heard them in real life when I taught this material in person to faculty on campuses. Right about now, the voices are saying something a little like this: "Tenure credit? What the heck is that?" "Tenure currency? I can have some of that? You're telling me I ALREADY have some of that?"

This is around the time in my workshops and presentations when the women faculty of color I meet really sit up and take notice, and I'm not going to try and hide it: This makes me VERY happy. Because YES, you have a bunch of currency already built up, YES you can reach into your proverbial super-invisible labor "purse" for that, and YES you already have credit in your name that you can put to use towards the things that matter to you—like retention, tenure, and promotion.

All we need to work on is how you claim that credit and currency and use it to your maximum benefit in reviews.

Don't get exploited thinking that invisible labor is benign and you just have to "shoulder" the additional weight. No! Don't listen to those who try to goad you into believing this inequitable work is how you should show your commitment to work, students, social justice, etc. Again: Just no. These are just lies and manipulation that will result in your demise.

It's heartbreaking enough that the statistics reveal this undue burden being carried by women faculty of color—but what's even more unspeakable is that this super invisible labor *frequently leads to failed tenure bids*. This is because this invisible overload of teaching service takes time away from you accumulating the currency that the university values (e.g., publications, grants). These things are what get rewarded in tenure reviews[5] and when you don't have those things (e.g., because you're delivering uncredited teaching excellence), the university will boot you out and show you the exit door.

And because this is one of the "Ahas" that can be hard to really grasp, I'll say it again more clearly and a bit louder for those in the back row: Super-invisible labor robs women faculty of color of the recognized currency needed to achieve retention, tenure, and promotion. This results in their failed retention, tenure, and promotion bids, and ends their academic career. Period.

Yep. Let the steam come out of your ears, because you don't want to hold that stuff in.

There is a better way. I don't say that flippantly, in some sort of rainbows and unicorns way. I can say that with conviction to you because I've seen it. Too often, women faculty of color will say, in retrospect, that they were "naive" about what the extra classroom labor would cost their careers. Perhaps you can relate to doing this extra work "without being asked," "because it was the right thing to do for students," and "at your expense." I hear these key phrases often, and I'm curious. What if I said you can take those phrases and swap them out with more empowering ones? Phrases like "having your invisible labor counted in your formal reviews," "turning teaching labor inequities into tenure gold," or even "taking and receiving your due credit towards promotion?" Would you believe that's possible?

If you're like the women faculty I've worked with over the last twenty years, I know you *want* to believe it's possible—you'd love to poke your chest out and claim your important contributions to your institution. Well, it's time to take that hope and make it a reality. I want you to clearly understand how to make sure that the super-invisible labor you provide to the university through your teaching is no longer ignored or overlooked. Let's make doubly sure you get the FULL credit that is owed to you in support of your tenure and promotion. You ready?

Well, read on, because that is my mission and where we'll get to by the end of this chapter.

Strategic Action:
Anchor Your Invisible Teaching Labor to Strong Points

The strategy to not get easily booted out or shown the exit by the university is to anchor fiercely to immovable objects, that is, to strong points. These strong points help you claim very visible credit towards tenure. When you do this, your currently super-invisible teaching labor becomes visible and therefore acknowledgable in your review materials.

Wondering what the heck I am talking about? Imagine you're in a storm—hurricane, tornado, whatever—and your survival depends on you not getting blown away. To survive and stay in place, you look around to identify what you can attach yourself to. And of course, you cannot just attach to any ol' thing. A young thin tree will not do. Nor will a street sign. You need a STRONG point to anchor to, like a building.

What I want to do now is provide you with two strong points—the two buildings—that can help you remain anchored in your role instead of being blown away, all the way out of your institution by the overwhelm of the super-invisible teaching labor you provide for their benefit.

Strong Point #1: The Language and Jargon of Teaching Outcomes

The common-sense understanding of students, colleagues, and society at large is that teaching is only about the transference of knowledge.[6] Well guess what? That everyday understanding is oh so very wrong.[7]

Women faculty of color's additional invisible labor comes from the fact that we know learning is about more than mere facts and figures.[8] Your teaching goes beyond the basics of knowledge acquisition—and that additional effort and value is what you must take credit for delivering.

Let's be clear: YOU, as a woman faculty of color, are the one who's delivering the learning outcomes to students that are essential.[9] This is according to research, employers, and the scholarship on teaching and learning. All of these sources make it plain that when it comes to teaching, women of color do it better. Yeah, I said it. Women faculty of color's teaching is just better. And I invite anyone to show me evidence to the contrary.

As women faculty of color, we know that we have to overperform to even be considered as equal to our peers.[10] And even when we don't aim to overperform, our experiences as diverse folks mean we approach the academy completely differently.[11] Our diverse lens means we don't see education as existing in a vacuum. We don't see knowledge as existing in a vacuum. And we bring that same diverse perspective to our teaching and classrooms.

The richness of diversity is what women faculty of color do in teaching often just by showing up.

> "What I'm trying to teach students is that there are different perspectives [in History] from the white male ones. Not just different perspectives in general, I mean different perspectives in terms of race and gender, **which I can speak to directly because of my lived experience.**"
> —Woman faculty of color History Professor

That is, the same diversity that research shows improves just about everything it touches—collaboration, innovation, workplace performance, productivity, etc.—also benefits our teaching as well.[12] So yeah, I said it, our teaching is just better.

Accordingly, we need to make sure that you are shining as bright as a diamond, rather than allowing your labor to keep getting sucked into a black hole. In this next section, I'm going to make sure you know how to anchor and highlight all of the special and essential extras that you do in your teaching—that is, your super-invisible teaching labor—by naming outright what you do using the SoTL's language, jargon, and description of what you do in your classrooms.

The SoTL is very clear. Students are not in our classrooms just to gain new knowledge. We're supposed to teach to provide a range of outcomes for students so that they develop as whole persons.[13] By looking at the many categories of student outcomes put forward by the varied bodies of scholarship (e.g., student development, teaching and learning, psychology, labor, etc.) you will discover language to claim and make visible your valuable yet super-invisible teaching labor on learning outcomes.

The most well-known and accepted categories of student outcomes are the American Association of Colleges and Universities' (i.e., AACU) Essential Learning Outcomes.[14]

As I describe the AACU outcomes below, you should consider: Which are familiar to you? Which are you hitting dead center in your teaching (whether you planned to do so or not)? Trust me, you'll be pleasantly surprised at all the wonderful things currently invisible in your teaching that are precisely what's considered exemplary. I'll make that explicit by describing what the research reveals as stellar about women faculty of color's teaching outcomes. And better yet, you'll be thrilled to be able to claim these in your retention, tenure, and promotion reviews. We did say tenure currency, did we not?

WHAT DO WOMEN FACULTY OF COLOR WANT STUDENTS TO KNOW BY THE END OF THEIR COURSES?

This is the category everyone presumes is the point of the classroom, and not just a point, but the main or only point. And we certainly hope every faculty on any campus achieves the traditional learning goal of transmitting content knowledge. It includes the information, theories, ideas, facts, formulas, etc. of the course subject and is called "**Knowledge of Human Cultures and the Physical and Natural World.**"[15] It includes:

- Sciences and mathematics
- Social sciences
- Humanities
- Histories
- Languages
- The arts

A few commonplace examples of knowledge course outcomes include answers to questions such as:

- *What makes the study of macroeconomics important?*
- *What place does literature have in the world outside of college?*
- *What are the basic principles of physics (e.g., Newton's laws of motion; mass, force, and weight)?*

The fact of the matter is that women faculty of color go beyond their dominant status peers by pursuing the above knowledge *and* also incorporating diversity into that knowledge.[16] So, more often than not, their extraordinary examples of the knowledge category might be expansions that improve the above knowledge:

- *What makes the study of macroeconomics important for LGBTQIA people of color?*
- *What place does literature have in the world outside of college for women of color?*
- *What are the basic principles of physics (e.g., Newton's laws of motion; mass, force, and weight)—and how have women and people of color played a role in this knowledge?*

And sometimes what women faculty of color teach is entirely distinct and unique as it is knowledge that was previously excluded or unexamined:

- *What's the economic impact of same-sex marriage policies for LGBTQIA people of color?*

- *How have people of color and women contributed to chemistry?*
- *How do the perspectives of the colonized fill gaps or upend the colonizers' histories?*

That is, women faculty of color are teaching the mainstream knowledge of their fields and also the more inclusive knowledge their fields often overlook or ignore. We will dive further into diverse content in Chapter 4, right around the corner.

WHAT DO WOMEN FACULTY OF COLOR WANT STUDENTS TO BE ABLE TO DO BY THE END OF THEIR COURSES?

Being able to do something specific as a result of your teaching is another outcome often referred to in the SoTL as a "skill." Specifically, most are familiar with what are referred to as the **Intellectual and Practical Skills**[17] listed here:

- Inquiry and analysis
- Critical and creative thinking
- Written and oral communication
- Quantitative literacy
- Information (e.g., digital) literacy
- Teamwork and problem solving

Several everyday illustrations of these course outcomes are items such as:

- Critical thinking about the knowledge being presented
- Communicate the course knowledge in writing and orally
- Ability to work in a team on course labs and projects
- Calculate a math problem or solve an equation

A lot of faculty would say that they encourage critical thinking, and support it as a learning outcome. However, research demonstrates that women faculty of color excel beyond their white and male peers as they teach these skills to students in connection to solving real-world problems[18] *and* to diversity as a whole in society.[19]

As a result, women faculty of color's exceptional outcomes for these skills might also look like this:

- Critical thinking to address real-world issues and challenges (especially those affecting diverse communities)
- Improved communication skills to improve (especially diverse) students' life chances (i.e., access to housing, education, health care, employment, etc.)
- Ability to work in (diverse) teams in the real-world (e.g., workplaces, community, etc.)

Zooming out for a moment, this is a get-real moment, okay? Students acquiring these skills can be a matter of life or death for diverse populations. And it can be a matter of life or death for the diverse students themselves. Any single student having their worldview developed in this way can influence the opportunities the students get access to in terms of housing, education, and health. These intellectual and practical skills are the opposite of theoretical to women faculty of color. Unlike your white counterparts, you're helping produce these skills in students specifically for the purpose of preparing them to solve real-world challenges and issues.

WHAT DO WOMEN FACULTY OF COLOR WANT STUDENTS TO BE ABLE TO CONTRIBUTE TO SOCIETY BY THE END OF THEIR COURSE?

Beyond the cognitive, numerical, communication, and problem-solving skills (i.e., intellectual and practical skills) above there are additional skills that may surprise you. These too are explicitly recognized in the SoTL, though your colleagues and students may not recognize them as such.

Below are the skills that women faculty of color have been particularly concerned with producing through their teaching.[20] Our consistent goals are for students to be active participants within democracy and to be ethical human actors. These and other similar outcomes are referred to as **Personal and Social Responsibility Skills**.[21]

- Civic knowledge and engagement—local and global
- Intercultural knowledge and competence
- Ethical reasoning and action
- Foundations and skills for lifelong learning

Women faculty of color are more likely to teach these skills to students.[22] When they do, it can look like:

- Civic knowledge and engagement—local and global:
  - *Knowledge about voter suppression of people of color, critical thinking and communication skills to offset and upend voter suppression.*
  - *Critical analysis of literature on the lived experience of women of color and other structurally oppressed groups.*
  - *Engaged citizenship advocating for science and shaping how research is applied in diverse communities.*
- Intercultural knowledge and competence:
  - *Intercultural skills for working in diverse STEM teams.*
  - *Anti-racist skills for providers such as teachers, dentists, social workers, doctors, nurses, etc.*
  - *Cultural knowledge necessary to coordinate community well-being efforts with diverse stakeholders.*
- Ethical reasoning and action:
  - *How to ethically cast performers in theater productions (e.g., without stereotyping or excluding racial groups).*
  - *Ethical considerations in pursuing science innovation (e.g., atomic bomb, stem cell research, essentializing minority groups, etc.).*
  - *Identifying moral reasoning justifications for unjust social and economic policy initiatives.*
- Foundations and skills for lifelong learning:
  - *Any learning activities that promote students' ongoing:*
    - *Curiosity*
    - *Transfer*
    - *Independence*
    - *Initiative*
    - *Reflection*

The AACU highlights that all these skill outcomes above should be "anchored in active involvement with diverse communities and real-world challenges"—exactly the manner in which you do it![23]

Finally, women faculty of color teach such that knowledge and skills are not abstract items unconnected to one another or disconnected from the real world's complex problems. When we have students use their new knowledge and skills in this manner[24] the essential outcome is referred to as **Integrative and Applied Learning**. This may look like:

- Apply mathematical equations to improve access to clean drinking water for impoverished communities (e.g., Flint, MI).
- Write a white or policy paper for a real-world issue (e.g., police violence against Blacks).
- Create a performance or art to demonstrate a social movement's aims (e.g., #MeToo).
- Design science and community collaborations to solve industrial pollution in a lower income neighborhood.

As shown in the examples above, we prepare students to contribute to society by having them apply their new knowledge and skills to a new situation. We teach students to bring all of the learning to home plate, that is, we teach students to apply ALL of the above essential learning outcomes[25] to "new settings and complex problems,"[26] often those with relevance to the real world.[27]

In other words, you do a lot of fabulous things you can claim credit for in your retention, tenure, and promotion reviews!

Alright, let's take a pause and let this sink in. Did you happen to recognize yourself in the above text? Perhaps you felt an eyebrow raise of recognition in more than one section. I, for one, am not at all surprised, however I would be remiss if I didn't pause and encourage you to celebrate, do a happy dance, or in some other way pat yourself on the back. You're doing a great job teaching in alignment with the excellent learning outcomes as set out by the SoTL.[28]

The next step in this strategic action is to use this language to get credit for your labor by explicitly writing about your teaching as focusing on these specific outcomes described in the SoTL, particularly in your materials for tenure and promotion.

> **For example, you can include a sentence that states** "my teaching focuses on the core learning goals in the scholarship of teaching and learning such as . . ." (and then list the learning outcome categories/goals below that apply to your teaching or course).
>
> **Knowledge of Human Cultures and the Physical and Natural World:**[29]
>
> - Sciences and mathematics
> - Social sciences
> - Humanities
> - Histories
> - Languages
> - The arts
>
> **Intellectual and Practical Skills:**[30]
>
> - Inquiry and analysis
> - Critical and creative thinking
> - Written and oral communication
> - Quantitative literacy
> - Information (e.g., digital) literacy
> - Teamwork and problem solving
>
> **Personal and Social Responsibility Skills:**[31]
>
> - Civic knowledge and engagement—local and global
> - Intercultural knowledge and competence
> - Ethical reasoning and action
> - Foundations and skills for lifelong learning
>
> **Integrative and Applied Learning:**[32]
>
> - Application of new knowledge and skills to a new situation

There, doesn't claiming credit for your teaching labor in reviews feel better than providing all that invisible teaching labor and having it all vanish into thin air?

And there you have it. Now you and your teaching are anchored to a rock-solid building in the middle of a storm. That's a win!

But let's get you anchored to another strong point, because why not? After all, there's a storm threatening our livelihood, well-being, and careers.

Strong Point #2: Breadth of Learning Outcomes (and also SoTL Minefield: Proceed with Eyes Wide Open)

The SoTL does a great job of naming and describing the core learning outcomes faculty should include in their teaching. As we've seen in the prior sections, there is a breadth and variety of the core learning outcomes that can be achieved in any given classroom. Simple, right? Just go out and put those learning outcomes into your course. Mmm . . . not quite. Unfortunately, it's not quite that simple.

As a proponent of many things in the SoTL, you will find me pointing to that research to help you strengthen your persistence and success in the university, to deepen your convictions about what you do, and to utilize the language that's recognized to communicate these things.

However, I'm not advocating for mindlessly swallowing these ideas whole. In the same way that all bodies of scholarship have holes in them, the scholarship of teaching and learning has its limits, and lets women of faculty of color down in key areas. This section is here to make sure you aren't caught unaware of its shortcomings.

In this case, the SoTL doesn't acknowledge that privilege and power rear their ugly heads when it comes to faculty choices in learning outcomes. And that is a huge omission that results in the SoTL leaving women faculty of color vulnerable. With this gap, women faculty of color walk into power dynamics unaware and unequipped.

Here's what I'd tell you if we were sitting together——Don't fall for the okey doke! The problem is that the majority of faculty are not engaging in the full range or breadth of these core learning outcomes, when they should be doing so.

Instead, according to research, most faculty (let's be real, given their overrepresentation, faculty means white male faculty) are engaging in only about half of them.

Specifically, their most common skill-related learning outcomes are:

- Written communication 90 percent
- Critical thinking and analytic reasoning 87 percent
- Oral communication 78 percent
- Quantitative reasoning 77 percent

In contrast, their least common learning outcomes are:

- (Information) digital literacy 29 percent
- Civic skills 34 percent
- Integrative learning 36 percent
- Working effectively in a team 37 percent

What happens when the majority of (white male) faculty are doing something? Given the power of the white and male statuses in society, what they do becomes the norm and standard by which others are judged.[33]

Here's what I am saying: The majority of white men in higher education are gatekeepers who set the standards of what is excellent and appropriate, and what is incompetent. As is the way with bias and power, those standards are based on their own experience and lenses[34] and do not include others—like you. What do you think that means in this context? If you said, "it means 'normal' and appropriate learning outcomes are the ones white male faculty uphold," you would be correct. And moreover, the learning outcomes white male faculty do not value or see as "normal"? These are the outcomes met with suspicion, the ones that are punished. And the faculty who focus on those "abnormal"—to them—outcomes? They're the faculty who are judged harshly.

And that is exactly what's happening to women faculty of color whose learning goals don't fit within the dominant white male norms. You are being punished, judged harshly, and treated with suspicion.[35]

The reality is that women faculty of color have excellent teaching as we frequently incorporate the breadth of the core learning outcomes.[36] But instead of being rewarded for teaching a full range of goals, we're being punished for engaging in the least common (yet clearly excellent) outcomes. In my decades of experience working with women of color faculty, here are common ways that student and colleague punishment and pushback to the less common learning outcomes show up:

> Dr. Renee Adeoye is a Black historian whose students use the colonial history of police in the U.S. to understand current police violence against Blacks and people of color. Her colleagues angrily tell her that history (e.g., knowledge) is neutral and should be taught as such. Students and colleagues admonish her teaching as biased and representing a "political agenda." All of this shows up as low ratings in the student evaluations and teaching observations used in her formal reviews.

What is wrong with this picture and how can we understand it better? Dr. Renee teaches the *integrative learning* goal of having students apply course content to real world problems. This integrative learning goal is clearly included, valued, and encouraged by the SoTL. So why the pushback? Because her classroom goal violates long-standing white male "norms." You know them well. They are the goals of (1) teaching knowledge for knowledge's sake and (2) viewing any "application" of said knowledge as an attempt to change society towards a "biased" lens.

Let's look at another common scenario:

> As an ethnomusicologist (someone who studies music in its social and cultural contexts) Assistant Professor Callie has her students work in groups to investigate music trends on social media. They identify if (and how) the trend

is cultural misappropriation of racial and ethnic minority music. In reviews of her teaching, Dr. Callie's colleagues protest that music trends on social media aren't "scholarly" or "real music" worthy of examination in a classroom. Despite evidence to the contrary, found in their group's work on cultural misappropriation, students label Dr. Callie as a racist in student evaluations with claims that music belongs to "everyone" along with complaints about having to work in groups.

What's going on here, and how can we understand this? It turns out, we can readily comprehend things when we just look at the AACU Essential Learning Outcomes.[37] In addition to having students apply concepts to real world context (e.g., integrative learning), Dr. Callie is also teaching students to:

- Work in a team to accomplish goals
- To know when there is a need for (digital) information, to be able to identify, locate, evaluate, and effectively and responsibly use and share that information for [a] problem at hand.[38]

While working in teams and (digital) information literacy are explicitly both valued by the SoTL[39] as well as employers,[40] these learning outcomes run counter to norms held by dominant students and colleagues. "Knowledge for knowledge's sake" is the key norm in academia. And yet, knowledge for knowledge's sake is not what employers want and request. Even though the SoTL specifies that knowledge and skills are to be practiced and applied to complex real-world problems,[41] women faculty of color are disciplined for teaching with these goals by thwarting their tenure with claims of bias or "inappropriate," "unscholarly," or "unnecessary/busywork" assignments.

Here is one final example of a best practice that is less common among white men. Heaven forbid that women of color actually teach students to participate in their communities and society.

You know, teaching students the AACU outcome of *civic skills*. Again, the white male norms of the academy as a place of "knowledge for knowledge's sake" views these aims as not scholarly or academic as they are not "purely" about the thinking (hu)man.

Yes, there are white men faculty and students who support and engage in civic skills as a classroom goal with glee. However, they often do so in the context of dominant ideas (e.g., governance principles) and context (e.g., political science students volunteering as poll workers). So they wouldn't even get questioned about encouraging civic skills or engagement.

But women faculty of color engage in civic skills as intended by the SoTL in that their classroom goal is "(a)nchored in active involvement with *diverse* communities and *real-world challenges*" (italics added)".[42]

Due to this inclusion and focus on civic skills with diverse communities (e.g., people of color) and on real-world challenges (e.g., voting disenfranchisement of Latinos and Blacks)—those with dominant statuses perceive this *civic skills* learning goal as women of color teaching biased content and having a political agenda and a focus on irrelevant and inappropriate aims[43]—rather than recognizing this labor as perfectly aligned with the SoTL's (1) definition of a "legitimate" and (2) best teaching practice.

The examples above illustrate that even when we're engaging in the best practices with our learning goals, when we violate the dominant normative (i.e., most common) learning goals–the white men who are in the position to set standards and assess us are formally evaluating our teaching as different, abnormal, and deficient.[44] Women faculty of color's teaching seems out of place because our goals exemplify the breadth of the best SoTL practices—while most others' teaching does not.[45] So even though our teaching outcomes aim exactly for what they should,[46] our teaching is met by hostility with claims of our teaching being incompetent and biased.[47] This is how women faculty of color's retention, tenure, and promotion bids[48] get killed, and our academic careers are cut short.

To fight back, hold fast to this anchor by referencing the SoTL "breadth" of learning outcomes as teaching excellence.

ANCHOR TO STRONG POINTS 57

> **For example, you might say or write something like:**
>
> My teaching reflects the *breadth* of learning outcomes like ____, ____, and ____ [list your learning outcomes that are less common for dominant faculty] which is recognized in the scholarship of teaching and learning as teaching excellence.
>
> Or:
>
> While many faculty's teaching is "one note/basic," focusing on a narrow swath of the most common learning outcomes (e.g., knowledge), my learning outcomes (____, ____, and ____ [list your learning outcomes that are less common for dominant faculty]) reflect the *breadth* recommended by the SoTL as a teaching best practice.

Foremost among the things missing in the SoTL is acknowledgment that women faculty of color aren't perceived—by students or colleagues—as having the expertise to choose their learning outcomes.

In this way, the SoTL misses the resistance and challenges these women face. When you think about it this way, you may be able to see that your breadth of learning goals and engagement in the less common goals—which seem normal, everyday, and traditional to you—may in fact be completely disrupting the expectations of your colleagues and students.

But still, anchor here to this building (i.e., breadth of learning outcomes to protect your less common learning outcomes), because their uninformed understanding is no match for the SoTL clarity that these ARE the excellent teaching outcomes and your engagement in the breadth of outcomes is stellar!

When the Rubber Hits the Road: Claiming Your Invisible Classroom Labor in Reviews

For all of the above reasons, it is vitally important for you to be explicit about the super-invisible teaching labor you provide. To claim that labor on your reviews you must make it:

1. *Visible* by anchoring to the *formal terminology, language, and yes, the scholarly jargon* in the scholarship of teaching and learning to <u>name</u> your <u>learning outcomes</u>, and
2. *Spotlighted* as stellar by anchoring to the fact that your specific and distinctive (i.e., less common) learning outcomes are *the embodiment of the <u>breadth</u> of learning outcomes touted as <u>teaching excellence</u>* by the scholarship of teaching and learning

And when I say explicit, I mean it. In my experience working with faculty, their teaching statements often include broad and vague philosophical statements about their teaching. Given that your extraordinary classroom labor is ignored *and* results in accusations of bias, incompetence, and illegitimate scholarship, you cannot submit review materials where you tiptoe, make subtle nods, or are modest about your learning outcomes. You must full-on brag in teaching materials with your (1) named and described learning outcomes and (2) accolades of teaching excellence for your breadth of (i.e., inclusion of less common) learning outcomes.

This strategy works because it makes it plain (1) that what you're doing in your classroom are actual learning outcomes and (2) that these learning outcomes are what you're supposed to be doing based on the scholarship of teaching. That your learning goals are not errant teaching, optional aims, "bias," nor an "agenda" but instead your invisible teaching labor serves nothing short of the excellence required for learning and for the purpose of higher education. That when you teach beyond just a knowledge-based goal, that's not just normal, but a best practice that should be widespread.

Your super-invisible labor that produces these impressive learning outcomes shouldn't be overlooked nor get pushback. You are a role model and I celebrate you as such.

Because your learning goals are a disruption to the status quo, there will still be resistance, and that's just a fact of life. A fact of life I hope you now feel much more empowered to face, while also claiming credit for your invisible teaching labor in your conversations with colleagues and in your review materials.

And that's it, you now have strong anchors that are the smart, friendly hands on your shoulders, holding you strongly in place. You no longer have to be the woman who does everything in her teaching, contributes extra for student benefit, and is unclear why that labor gets ignored and villainized, making everything feel so hard. You're on your way to the more empowered way of operating in your classroom and in your retention/tenure/promotion reviews that I want most for you. Congratulations!

Summary

I hope this chapter comes across as a kind of energetic up-level, and that after reading it you have an empowered sense of your teaching excellence via your learning outcomes. To encourage you to make these learning outcomes visible so they can be counted in your reviews, remember:

- Your and WFOC's super-invisible teaching labor produces stellar learning outcomes for students.
- Make your super-invisible teaching labor visible by anchoring to the SoTL language of "learning outcomes" to expand the perception of value you bring to your institution and classroom.
- Your and WFOC's chosen learning outcomes are anchored to the teaching excellence of "breadth" as defined by the scholarship on teaching and learning, driving undeniable reasons for university buy-in.

60   CHAPTER 2

- The SoTL falls short by failing to account for the unique classroom and career challenges WFOC face when implementing excellent learning outcomes.
- You must take ownership of the visibility of your valuable super-invisible teaching labor and teaching excellence by explicitly claiming it in your retention, tenure, and/or promotion materials.

Empowering Actions You Can Take This Week

I want you to not just make your contributions visible, I want you to shout it out and brag. And I don't mean a humble brag either. Show them that you're providing the teaching labor, learning outcomes, and excellence that cannot be disputed.

So be bold! Share your most important "Ahas" in public, #empoweredWFOC on the social media platform of your preference so we can connect more and share with each other.

1. What's the main idea you want to retain from this chapter about your learning outcomes?
2. Which category of learning outcomes do you now realize you aim for?
3. Have a look at your teaching for the next week. Which learning outcome can you simply and easily add more of, or perhaps just make it more visible by simply stating it explicitly to your students? And colleagues?
4. If this chapter stirred up emotions about the challenges you've experienced with resistance towards your learning goals, take ten minutes to express that discontent and, if appropriate, anger or grief. Do so with a fellow WFOC or in a safe space such as a journal or with me at empowered@effectivefaculty.org.
5. Finally, who can you share your shifts about your learning outcomes with? Is it a fellow WFOC, or a receptive colleague? Maybe you're on social media and want to quote something from the above, or make a declaration

of your own? A public step like this can be scary, but it can also be a rush.

Congratulations on rejecting burnout and invisible labor. I'm excited for you to get your teaching labor visible and counted in your reviews! Next up, we're going to dive into how to protect yourself from confusing or negative student interactions so you can stop having your energy drained and your adrenaline on high on a daily basis, with negative consequences for your career. See you in the next chapter.

Chapter 3

BUILD A PROTECTIVE AND NURTURING BUBBLE

Master how to develop an empowered space for your teaching and academic career.

Reclaim your classroom from the confusing, harsh, and distracting student interactions that unfairly plague women faculty of color.

△ *Dr. Yvonne Johnson's African American literature class session is about to start, and she's visualizing all of the things she's getting ready to walk into. There's Jennifer, the student who throws daggers at her with her eyes. John, who barges into her office and invades her physical space after assignments are returned to protest his grade, is sure to sit front and center, as he has in every class so far. And Robert is sure to verbally attack her for every assigned reading, discussion question, and research fact she'll use to teach today.*

She still isn't sure which student(s) turned her in to Professor Watch, or reported her to the Dean for teaching about structural racism as faced by characters in the assigned books for this class. She had to have security walk her to class for a month until the online hate mail and doxxing subsided. And she wonders . . . will today be the day another "pop-up" observer arrives to surveil her teaching at the behest of the Dean?

Semester after semester, week after week, and one class session after another—like Groundhog day—Yvonne has dreaded this ever-present intensity in class. She spends an inordinate amount of time course prepping hoping to reduce student drama. Teaching is so draining that she's too tired to do any research or writing, before or afterwards. Not to mention grading and student evaluation season, which turns up her anxiety, anger, fear, and resignation because students use them as an opportunity to bully and punish her.

But guess what? These days, even though she's facing the same minefield of a classroom day after day, year after year—there she goes . . . bubbling over with calm, peace, security, and a pep in her step. She's got this, and so can you. Let's talk about how it's done, with—trust me on this—a little something called classroom management. △

Strategic Action:
Classroom Management Isn't What You Think It Is

You're probably thinking "Say what now?!" and wondering how you can walk into a war zone with pep in your step. Or, you may flat-out think it's impossible. No, it's completely possible for you to feel empowered in a classroom that looks like Dr. Yvonne's, or worse for that matter, because we're not sugar-coating how bad things can get. Now if you're asking "Okay exactly how does it work?," read on, because the SoTL strategy of classroom management is what makes it happen.

I know there's long-standing resistance to even thinking about classroom management, not to mention implementing it. Before we tackle that, let's first get clear on what classroom management is (and is not):

Classroom management is a term that includes the broad range of strategies faculty use to ensure their classroom runs smoothly, so it's an environment conducive to teaching and learning.

I'm guessing that's not quite what you thought I was going to say, right? I like to ground people with a definition of classroom management FIRST so it's clear we're talking about classroom strategies for learning. Learning in a classroom is about more than just the pedagogy or teaching. It's also about setting up, modeling, and maintaining an environment in which faculty can teach—that's you—and students can learn. Done right, you can think of classroom management as your new best friend.

Furthermore, classroom management can be described as a wheel with spokes, each of which calls for implementation: Classroom layout, time management, instruction, relationship-building, policies and procedures, materials, and behavior management.[1]

The best-case scenario to proactively create a hospitable classroom is to implement each classroom management spoke using evidence-based strategies. But who has that kind of time and energy on top of already existing overloads and pressures? Certainly not you as a disproportionately burdened woman of color faculty member,[2] so I have a proposition for you.

You can go back and implement other strategies later, but right now you must implement the single most overlooked area—the one that provides the most bang for your buck. Ironically, it's also the area your colleagues are most likely actively turning their nose up about: Behavior management.

Behavior Management Is a Best Practice, Not an Optional One

In order to create a classroom environment in which you can teach (and students can learn), and because I want you to see a tangible difference as swiftly as possible, in this chapter we're going to focus on behavior management. The goal is that by taking the action steps at the end of the chapter, you will see a measurable difference in how you think about behavior management leading to more pep in your step. The most straightforward and effective manner to implement behavior management is to share behavior expectations with students.[3]

Keeping in mind the spokes on the classroom management wheel, your use of behavior expectations as a strategy is to simply inform students of the behaviors necessary in your classroom for it to run smoothly. Doing this, you create an environment conducive for you to teach and students to learn. No more. No less.

Again, classroom management and behavior management are not optional or only for "bad," "incapable," or so-called "authoritative" teachers. They are mandatory for good teaching:

> "If you ask me to pick the single most critical issue that new instructors should focus on, it would be classroom management . . .
>
> Indeed, for new college educators to survive and flourish, one of the most important things they need to do is consistently establish and manage student expectations and behavior . . .
>
> As instructors, we forget just how confusing it is for students who travel from class to class and encounter differences and inconsistencies," says Saunders, noting that it's important to not only communicate your expectations but to frame them in such a way that students understand the rationale behind the behaviors you're requesting.[4]

Simply put, behavior expectations should be developed and communicated by all faculty in all of their courses. All of our courses are different and students are not mind readers. So you have to be transparent with them about the behaviors that support *and disrupt* the teaching and learning in your course.[5]

Here are some of the evidence-based benefits of a behavior-expectations teaching practice according to the extensive classroom management literature:[6]

- Students understand and engage in the range of learning supportive behaviors
- Allows the majority of classroom time to be spent on instructional activities
- Increases the amount of time students are immersed in learning
- Little time spent managing student behaviors
- Minimized student distractions and disruptions from learning
- Less of the teacher drain and stress required by having to deal with student misbehavior
- Reduced frequency and intensity of behavioral problems
- Increase comfort and enjoyment in the learning environment for everyone

Back to the pep in Dr. Yvonne's step? Firmly heading off a hostile classroom environment—disruptions, incivilities, harassment, discriminations, aggressions, etc., you know the drill—is how you create a bubble of protection. Call it a pep in your step, a float in your boat, or a little joy in your day, that bubble of protection is what empowers you to thrive, and in case you hadn't noticed, your empowerment is number one here in this book, on my watch.

Key Features of Behavior Expectations Statements

Classroom management and behavior management involves multiple moving pieces but let's get the first essential piece in place, that is, a statement of classroom behavior expectations. When I mention a statement for behavior expectations, you may think of something like this:

Dr. Bob Colby is an instructor of philosophy who asks his students to abide by the "Golden rule—treat others as you would like to be treated."

"Students are to interact with one another with respect" is what is written in Dr. Smith's syllabus for a course in the Fine Arts program.

And Dr. Claire Monroe expects students to behave "civilly" in her chemistry classroom.

I will say straight out—not only are these the classroom interaction guidelines of privileged faculty—but they are not effective because they are not in line with the SoTL. These sorts of statements of classroom behavior expectation are vague and hollow, pretty much leaving how students behave in the classroom open to their interpretation of cultural norms and social status.

Having said that, don't panic or feel embarrassed if your guidelines look similar. Many of us learned to teach by modeling those who taught us in graduate school. And those folks were primarily white males, correct? In that context, the teaching norms established for others reflect privileged social statuses. It may help you to know that you're not alone if you have similar expectations for your classroom as those above. Through my consulting work with institutions and individual faculty, I have read hundreds of these statements and the bulk of them are of this vague type. In other words, they provide no protection or safeguard for a classroom climate where students can learn and women faculty of color can teach.

So what is an *effective* Classroom Behavior Expectations Statement? Now that we've talked about the wrong way to do it, let's switch to talking about how you can put together effective guidelines for classroom behavior. In short, effective guidelines have all (not one or some, but all) of the following features:[7]

- *Feature #1: Clear statement of behavior expectations*
- *Feature #2: Examples of what behaviors are encouraged and discouraged*
- *Feature #3: Consequences for behaviors that disrupt and distract the learning environment*

Let's address each of these in a little more detail, with the goal of you being able to at least start on these yourself.

Feature #1: Clear Statement of Behavior Expectations

A clear statement of behavior expectations is a broad description of how learning occurs in your classroom. It explains to students how your effective learning environment looks. This feature is what folks think of when they hear "behavior expectations." Remember those vague examples I gave above (e.g., respect, do unto others, civility)? They are actually illustrations of this specific feature.

Stating what's valued in your classroom (e.g., respect, civility) is necessary to set the vibe and tone of your learning environment to students. The problem is that most faculty stop there. But to do so leaves your behavior management ineffective—it is too vague for students to follow, it leaves the behaviors up to student interpretation, and it requires students to read your mind about what you mean.

We'll use (and build upon) an abbreviated illustration to demonstrate each of the necessary features for classroom interaction.

> **Brief Illustration of Feature #1:**
>
> *For this class to be effective, you must be an active participant. So that we can all learn from each other, we must treat each other with respect.*

In this brief illustration we've told students that our classroom is one where engagement, active (not passive) learning, and respect in our treatment of others are valued. We've also said that these are valued because they promote learning (i.e., to be effective; to learn from each other).

Note here that already this example is clearer than saying "Here we follow the Golden Rule," which brings up more questions than answers, and creates more othering than belonging.

Feature #2: Examples of What Behaviors Are Encouraged and Discouraged

Your classroom behavior expectations must explicitly tell students the behaviors that are encouraged and discouraged or prohibited in your classroom. Feature #1 lets students know the important values, principles, disposition, etc. that are important for learning. But alone, it kind of means nothing. It is pie in the sky language that is open to interpretation. That is why the prior feature must be accompanied by this one, which makes plain the specific behaviors required to succeed in your classroom.

Continuing to build up on our illustration, let's add individual behaviors to the broad ideas of "active" and "respect":

> **Brief Illustration of Feature #2:**
>
> *To be an active participant in this classroom means that you contribute to each class session, ask questions, answer others' questions, add relevant information to the conversation or task at hand, and not demand passive learning.*
>
> *Respect in our classroom means that you follow faculty directions for learning activities, not interfere with others' ability to contribute, and do not put down others' contributions to the class session.*

In this brief illustration, "active participation" is defined with three encouraged and one discouraged behavior. And "respect" is defined with one encouraged and two discouraged behaviors.

At least initially, this amount of detail may seem like overkill. But please let me remind you that students are going from classroom to classroom with faculty making similar statements about "respect" and "participation." Participation in another faculty member's class could look completely different from yours depending on your pedagogy, discipline, class size, etc. For example, are students to shout out, or raise their hands?

This is why it is important to guide students towards the behaviors that support (and don't disrupt) learning in YOUR classroom. This feature essentially is you translating the broader philosophical concepts from your initial statement into specific actionable behaviors for students. For clear expectations and a protective bubble of empowered teaching for you—the detail matters.

We're not done just yet so stay with me. The final feature is just as important as the first two, if not more important.

Feature #3: Outcomes for Behaviors That Support or Disrupt the Learning Environment

Of course you will highlight and reward the students who abide by the behavior expectations. But here is the feature that many faculty don't want to do . . . but must: Include the possible outcomes for students if they behave in ways that disrupt your classroom. This feature transforms your mere words on a page into living, breathing, and actionable behavior expectations. Without this feature, students will realize they can ignore your expectations and engage in whatever behaviors they like. And when they engage in these disruptive behaviors, they aren't just annoying/scary/exhausting—they also disrupt your ability to teach and other students' ability to learn. And isn't that why you're in the classroom in the first place? To provide instruction so that students can learn? In that case, you must have a mechanism to provide reinforcement—positive and negative—for the behaviors that support and detract from learning in your classroom. This will go far in creating the peace you long for in your classrooms, and let's face it, it's part of your job.

It's easy to think about how you might model and praise students who engage in learning supportive behaviors. As faculty, we have less experience with and knowledge about our options for disruptive behaviors.

Continuing our brief illustration, here is what this feature might look like:

> **Brief Illustration of Feature #3:**
>
> *The primary purposes of our classroom are teaching and learning, and our behavior expectations serve to foster an environment in which both can flourish. Student behaviors that support our learning environment will be rewarded and reinforced. This also means that behaviors that discourage or disrupt teaching and learning must be addressed. Failure to live up to these behavior expectations carries with it the possibility of sanctions, up to and including removal from a class, removal from a program, and/or removal from the university.*

In this brief illustration your students are reminded that the behavior expectations exist to foster teaching and learning. It also informs students of the outcomes of behaviors that both support or disrupt the learning environment. Hopefully this brief illustration demonstrates that this feature is nowhere near as dramatic as people fear, worry, and imagine. Simple. Straight to the point. Keep it moving. Nothing to see here.

And that is the three-step process I recommend you apply to creating a Classroom Behavior Expectations Statement. If you simply take the examples, string them together, and adapt as needed, you've further reinforced your empowered force field. This statement aids a healthy environment for your teaching and should be displayed as teaching excellence in your reviews. Do it this week. You won't be sorry.

Threat:

Incivilities and Their Consequences—Why You Must Enact This Strategy Even if You Don't Want To

Even though I've laid out this beautiful, proven strategy with evidence about its learning benefits, I suspect you still may not want to enact it. Chalk it up to over a decade of experience working intimately with women faculty of color like you. It's certainly understandable, but you really must do it. It pains me when I encounter faculty who still aren't doing this. Why? The reality is that women faculty of color are more likely to have classroom environments where students are hostile. So you have to have a proactive rather than a reactive approach.

Standards of Classroom Interaction Are Necessitated by the Well-Researched Reality—Women Faculty of Color Are More Likely to Have Classrooms Made Hostile by Students

Sometimes we need to know how bad the situation is before we take action. Sometimes we don't realize we are one woman in a wide swath of women just like us, and this is a bigger problem than "just us" having a "bad day." To that I offer you the research:

Students disrupt our teaching with inappropriate challenges to our classroom authority.[8] Students don't believe or acknowledge the credentials of women faculty of color.[9] We are not given the authority that white men receive from the start without question.[10] Instead we have to exert incredible amounts of thought, energy, and effort to secure "students' cooperation,"[11] to establish the credibility and authority we need to teach and have a successful learning environment.

Students aggressively question our teaching skill and competency[12] via attacks on our syllabi,[13] reading lists,[14] grading,[15] and a general "eagerness to jump on any little mistake or to find flaws in [our] logic to prove the incompetence students presume."[16]

We often describe feeling physically unsafe[17] because of students' hostile behaviors toward us,[18] their screaming at us,[19] and arguing and storming out with the impression they will return to our classroom as a campus shooter,[20] etc. And lately we have had to bear the brunt of disgruntled students making us targets online such that we are on the receiving end of doxxing and threats of violence from an even bigger anonymous audience.[21]

Consequences of Unchecked Classroom Incivilities

Classroom incivilities, microaggressions, macro-aggressions, harassment, discrimination, disruptions, anti-Black, anti-immigrant, etc. I'm not wedded to how you describe what's going on in your classroom. But I am wedded to you understanding that this classroom environment and these sorts of incidents are not good for learning, they're definitely not good for your well-being, and odds are they are—slowly, swiftly, or somewhere in between—killing your career.

Classroom incivility is not benign or without consequences. Attempts to brush off or hide your classroom incivility will not work—word of it inevitably gets out to your colleagues and manifests negatively in your student evaluations and retention/tenure/promotion reviews. Even in its mildest forms, student incivility reduces student learning and inhibits the effectiveness of faculty members' teaching.[22] In its most severe forms, in addition to losses in student learning and faculty teaching effectiveness, experiencing student classroom incivility can result in stressful workplace environments, job loss, and dire health consequences.

As you are no doubt well aware, student incivilities can also keep us from being effective teachers (or being perceived as such by students).[23] Student incivilities lead to lowered teaching evaluation scores, especially for us as women faculty of color in comparison to white women or men, as well as men of color faculty.[24] From there, this slippery slope leads to colleagues, chairs, and deans using these biased evaluations tainted by incivilities to deny our tenure and promotion. And to think, this can all get much better when you manage and reduce your classroom incivilities based on proven pedagogical practices like the Behavior Expectations Statement.

Women faculty of color know this truth in their bones, but the research also shows that prolonged and frequent experiences in classrooms toxic with student incivility might be linked to stress, burnout, disillusionment, lowered morale, desire to leave academia, and negative physical and mental health outcomes.[25] And of course, we spend a disproportionate amount of time in this environment given that faculty with our marginalized statuses (e.g., women of color) are allocated larger teaching loads than our mainstream peers.[26] If you've been sensing that the system is against you in this regard, that's because it is.

Be Proactive About Classroom Incivilities—They Are Not Benign

Let me say this in a very direct way so there is no misunderstanding: Student incivilities are not something you can pretend don't exist. You might think no one else knows your dirty little secret, that students can be just terrible in your class! No. It's known by others. Why? Students who lash out at you in your classroom also lash out when they are filling out your student evaluations. They also lash out when they are complaining about you in their other classes—to students in and professors of those courses. And they lash out at you in their close conversations with your colleagues with whom they are doing research, independent or directed study, etc. What you think is something only you know, simply isn't.

You may attempt to ignore student incivility and hope it'll stay quiet. But it isn't quiet in the first place. Let me invite you to ask yourself these questions: Is your head buried in the sand while students are painting you as a horrible teacher? Do you think they're out there owning up to their inappropriate uncivil behavior? What they don't realize, and what institutions mostly don't realize, is these are not benign lashing outs . . . unfounded unfavorable student evaluations are how your teaching will be reviewed for retention, tenure, and promotion. Colleagues hearing negative student chatter about your teaching are providing input to other colleagues, which leads to their negative votes when you are up for review. And that's what I mean when I say student incivility is not benign—it hurts your teaching, reputation, career, and health.

One of the most common mindset challenges I encounter in my work with women faculty of color is this: "Oh student incivilities are the least of my worries. They'll go away on their own." I'm here to empower you with candor, that is simply not true. Have you heard the saying "for want of a nail, the kingdom was lost?" Sad to say, but "for want of classroom management, entire academic careers can be lost."

The good news is this: You can and you MUST implement the behavior expectation strategy I teach above. Establish its three key features starting right away and from there improved student evaluations, teaching reviews, career, and mental and physical wellness all become possible.

But improved student evaluations and less colleague gossip about teaching aren't guaranteed. And thankfully those biased items aren't the main reason you are using this strategy. Nope. The real reason you are using the behavior expectations are to protect you from classroom toxicity AND provide you protection from the biased student and colleague mess come review time since: (1) your use of a research-based strategy provides evidence of you as a good teacher (make sure to say so in your review materials) and (2) you'll be able to frame biased students as violating your behavior expectations and disrupting learning (to counter the student evaluations and gossip narrative of you as a bad teacher). Protective bubble indeed!

SoTL Minefield:
What's Lacking and Lurking About Classroom Management

There is so much good that we can use in the SoTL about classroom management, and I hope you use every bit of that to uplift your experience of the classroom right away. The SoTL is crystal clear that behavior management, as part of classroom management, is a necessary and evidence-based strategy for student learning. They are also clear, however, that behavior management should not ONLY be enacted IF there are already pre-existing student disruptions. Rather, it is a preventative and proactive strategy to head off and address student incivility. It also isn't a practice for the so-called deficient or "troubled" faculty member. ALL faculty should be engaging in this practice, which makes it normative. In proactive and enlightened institutions, all students should be informed of and required to abide by the classroom behaviors each faculty has determined as supportive of their classroom. In these ways, when it's implemented, the SoTL makes it easy for women of color to feel at ease to enact this strategy. At the same time, there are two ways in which the scholarship of teaching and learning falls short for women faculty of color. Let's make sure you're aware of them so you don't fall victim to these shortcomings.

The Surprising Way the SoTL Ignores Race and Blames Women Faculty of Color for Incivilities

While the SoTL has long examined classroom incivilities,[27] it has given very little specific attention to women faculty of color's experiences of them. Surprisingly, classroom incivility literature has a track record of either ignoring faculty statuses altogether or claiming that faculty race and gender have no bearing on classroom incivilities. Say what now? The unfortunate truth is, like so many other fields of study, the SoTL suffers from a lack of nuance—all faculty experiences are not the same.

Here is one misguided example in a review of classroom incivility research:

> "In sum, although faculty attributes (e.g., race, gender, experience) are often argued to be associated with incivility, empirical support more consistently points to instructor behaviors (e.g., immediacy) and teaching methods.[28]

Please be sure to catch the last sentence—where it says that faculty are themselves to blame for student incivility. Umm, okay. This is what we need to be equipped to refute.

Whether realized or not, student incivility research has activated blame-the-victim logic against women of color faculty. It argues that race and gender are not relevant in student incivility—that women faculty of color's own behavior causes it. My guess is you're already saying this with me, with indignation and outrage: In what world do race and gender dynamics get left at the classroom door?

It's the twenty-first century, and everyone should know that race and gender simply cannot be excised from the context, no way, no how. In a sense, the SoTL is simply no different in its lack of awareness or ignorance. Having said that, it's our job to recognize where the research fails, or rather, I've made it my job so that you don't have to do it. But now that you see it laid out plainly, you get to bring this clarity with you as you create change for yourself in your classrooms. Race and gender cannot be separated from how a faculty member experiences student behavior in the classroom. Every faculty member—yes, that's you—brings all of themselves into the classroom.

As for instructor immediacy? Before we can even talk about student perceptions of immediacy, cross-race perceptions in general are heavily influenced by race and gender[29]. For example, research demonstrates that white individuals cannot accurately read nor interpret the facial expressions of racial minorities.[30] Instead, white individuals misattributed those persons' emotions, intent, etc. So if we know cross-race perceptions are influenced by race, of course we know students' perceptions of instructor immediacy—often referred to as "instructor warmth" and "instructor approachability"—will be as well. Again, there is no way to leave race and gender outside the classroom.

Further, there are deeply embedded societal stereotypes of women of color's "approachability" and "warmth" in particular, which are also entirely present in the classroom, brought in by the students themselves. Black women as mammies, Latinas expected to "mother," Asian "tiger moms,", etc.—and the shared stereotype of "sassiness" for subgroups within these women of color.[31] Each of these stereotypes is related to students' expectations of warmth and approachability for women of color and influences their behavior in class. This is a lose–lose situation for women of color who are punished by students both when they do and don't fulfill these stereotypes for them. You begin to see why I am so insistent, and loud, and persistent about implementing behavior and classroom management strategies. They are simply not optional, period.

In short, the SoTL research that renders race and gender invisible is woefully lacking and genuinely harmful to the cause of equity and inclusion on your campus. I urge you to take what's useful and apply it, but miss me with the misinformation that student incivilities are not related to faculty race and gender. As much as the SoTL has missed the boat on this, let's look forward to the day very soon when it fills in these holes.

The Truth about Classroom Experiences for Women Faculty of Color: Your Teaching Is NOT Deficient

I hope it's clear, I've made it my business to make sure women faculty of color do not believe the negative and inaccurate narrative about themselves. So let me tell you directly: Do not cosign the idea that your teaching is deficient. Even if you don't currently feel secure in the classroom, or feel that you can improve—don't blame yourself for structural inequality. You are not causing or deserving of the incivilities, classroom disruptions, hostile environment, toxic environment, whatever you want to call it that you might be facing in the classroom. This is why in a prior section in this chapter I taught you what is in the non-SoTL literature about student incivilities in our classrooms.[32] Women faculty of color are more likely than their privileged faculty colleagues to experience student:

- Inappropriate challenges to their authority
- Resistance to identity-related course content
- Accusations of teaching skill incompetence
- Threats to their career
- Threats to their physical safety
- Threats to their privacy

This is what's true about your experience. To pretend otherwise—whether that's a person denying this or the SoTL claiming race is irrelevant—is insulting, invalidating, and gaslighting.

You are not imagining things. You are not alone:

> Most faculty would not normally expect to be harassed by students. However, the women faculty of color interviewed for my study described interactions in which they felt devalued, challenged, and threatened by white male students. As Cathy says,
> "I sense my own vulnerabilities. So, I mean, it's like a policewoman, right? Or a woman soldier, right? Oh, you're going to get raped, you know?"
> This poignant quote encapsulates her view of what it feels like to be a woman of color in higher education—to have an esteemed status (e.g., PhD or professorship) but not the safety and authority that should come with it.
> That is, Cathy notes that being a professor should protect her from abuse from her white male students—yet she knows that this role cannot and does not protect her from the consequences of their gender and race privilege (i.e., being assaulted).[33]

Thankfully, research in other fields such as sociology, history, political science, etc. have made it clear that women of color experience classroom incivilities caused by student reactions to our race and gender[34] and that those incivilities can look a bit different from what is traditionally examined in the SoTL.[35] That is, we are experiencing structural oppression rather than suffering from individual deficit.

Okay. Time to take a deep breath and take these truths on board. Being empowered and, dare I say, even joyful on a daily basis in your career in academia starts with understanding what is real. Then with your feet on the ground based in reality, you can take empowered action to protect your academic career.

Meanwhile, there is just one more place the SoTL falls short.

The SoTL Ignores the Privilege and Power Inherent in Classroom Management

While classroom management has long been an essential evidence-based practice in the scholarship of teaching, classroom management in the SoTL also suffers from rare discussions of the structural privilege and power faculty must have to effectively enact this practice.

A lot of your privileged faculty colleagues don't understand that teaching requires that students recognize faculty authority. Instead, they are busy judging those who use sound teaching practices to establish authority (e.g., criticizing women of color faculty who require students to call them Dr.) or pretending to give privilege away (e.g., asking students to call them by their first name).

As I've mentioned elsewhere, teaching authority doesn't mean authoritative; it merely means that you have the duty—and right—to make the decisions for the classroom. That includes the teaching authority to shape the classroom environment so it is conducive to learning (e.g., Behavior Expectations Statement). While you might still get challenged by students in the classroom, this specific evidence-backed practice will both reinforce your empowered force field and provide you with the power to address it.

One final point about the potential role of privileged faculty in creating empowered classrooms for everyone: Privileged faculty should have effective classroom management in place as well, even if they "feel" it is unnecessary to do so. Often, their statuses make their authority a default, and they're imbued with "the golden touch" such that they feel as though they don't have to lay out behavior expectations as plainly. And the SoTL not discussing power and privilege leaves these faculty feeling as though it's okay to not engage in explicit classroom management and behavior expectations. Defaulting to what their privileged status gives them is the easy way out. But it ultimately does not make for an empowered campus where behavior expectations are the norms since they are in fact the best practice. Either way, their perfectly working force field affords them the ability to ignore this strategy. But YOU want to and must practice classroom management.

Empowered Possibilities for a Nurturing and Protective Bubble for Your Academic Career:
Which Dr. Rosa Will You Be?

Let's envision the following scenarios . . . first:

Scenario #1:

Dr. Rosa didn't have an effective policy for students' classroom interactions. She spent years in a classroom with toxic incivilities. Those incivilities bred more incivilities, seeped into student evaluations, and leaked into colleagues' informal chatter—cementing the narrative that she was a bad teacher. The incivilities and negative perception of her teaching has been so draining she hasn't been able to get her scholarship completed. And now with low research productivity, low morale, and low student evaluations scores, she is up for review.

Now take a look at this one . . .

Scenario #2:

Dr. Rosa had an effective policy for students' classroom interactions. It took energy for her to use it but she was able to nip most student incivilities in the bud. A few students channeled their incivility instead into evals and informal chatter with her colleagues. But she was able to defuse those with colleagues by discussing this (evidence-backed) policy to make it plain how she protects the learning environment. To her colleagues, she was able to confidently highlight classroom incivilities as student challenges to her behavior expectations and her classroom authority. With student incivilities in check, Rosa had energy and time to focus on her scholarship and personal well-being. Now she's up for review with healthy scholarly productivity under her belt and she looks forward to writing about this evidence-backed policy as evidence of her teaching prowess.

Imagine that you are Dr. Rosa. If you were her... which of these two scenarios makes you feel at ease? At risk? The one that makes your nerves bad and has you wringing your hands? Which scenario has you feeling settled and confident? Which one feels like more of a threat to your review? Presents you as a bad teacher and unproductive researcher? The one that could actually end your career by causing you to receive a negative review?

My goal for you is to be the faculty member in Scenario #2, with evidence-based practices in place offsetting inappropriate student challenges to your authority. We want nothing short of that, reclaiming your research productivity, well-being, and more.

The point I'm making is that once you put in place behavior expectations for your classroom, you will have your protective bubble and force field. You'll be able to exist in that learning space in a healthy manner. You'll have empowered your career. And most of all, you'll be able to walk into the classroom without worrying about what's coming your way.

Summary

By now you know what's real about your classroom. You know it's not your fault and you're not imagining things. You're not alone, and you have concrete examples of how to put behavior management in place to keep your teaching and academic career as protected as possible. What else is important to take away from this chapter? Here's a recap you can come back to whenever you need a boost to keep taking action to get and remain empowered in your teaching:

- Don't accept your classroom as a hostile and toxic environment. It can absolutely be better than you imagine.
- Instituting behavior expectations (classroom management) is a best practice, not an optional one or only for "bad" teachers. Note it as such on your reviews.
- There IS a right and wrong way to do behavior expectations, and you can do it RIGHT! Get your protective bubble in place!

- You and WFOC are more likely to experience student classroom incivilities, disruptions, harassment, etc.
- Behavior expectations are a must for you and WFOC. Behavior expectations are how you can breathe and thrive amidst toxic air!
- The SoTL erroneously denies that your and WFOC's lived classroom experiences are negatively impacted by privilege and power.
- You must design and launch your behavior expectations strategy to claim your own protective bubble to safeguard your teaching and reviews. Do it. You won't regret it.

Empowering Actions You Can Take This Week

A little transparency. I wish we could discuss this to make sure the key points land. But this is a book, so for now I'll do the next best thing and offer you a little added support through the items below to help the ideas sink in and your next actions take shape. Feel free to share your most important "Ahas" in public if you wish, and use hashtag #empoweredWFOC on the social media platform of your preference, so we can connect more and share with each other.

1. What's one "Aha!" moment you got about your understanding of classroom behavior expectations from reading this chapter?
2. Which of these small actions will you take today after reading this chapter?
   a. Be sure to look at your own campus policies to get a feel for the behavior expectations already in place for various aspects of students' campus life. These might be for residence halls, dining halls, public events, classrooms, sporting events, etc. This examination should make clear this is already quite a common and normative practice.
   b. Spend some time imagining, discussing with fellow WFOC, or just journaling: What would your

classroom look like without student incivilities? Feel like? How might your teaching experiences change? What would you do with that reclaimed energy and time? Use it on publishing? Grants? Family? Friends? Etc.
  c. Draft one sentence for each of the three key components of behavior expectations.
  d. Are you ready to adopt your newly revised classroom behavior expectations in your class? If not, what help do you need to go for it?
3. Do you have behavior expectations in place and in use but now need more advanced "in the moment" strategies? I'd love to hear from you to take this further, so email me: empowered@effectivefaculty.org.

Well done! This is an essential chapter. You did it. You and your career are now empowered by the nurturing bubble you've created with the protection of the SoTL. Now ... go ahead and exhale a big ol' sigh of relief. What's next? We're going to dive into the exciting topic of what you teach where you get to feel all warm inside and are rewarded in retention/tenure/promotion reviews for your fantastic teaching. Let's keep going because this is going to prove illuminating!

Chapter 4

THEY DON'T "GET IT" (AND THAT'S NOT REQUIRED)

Proudly display your course material as stellar, full of value and superb teaching!

Ensure your course content, topic, or material isn't underappreciated, viewed as unscholarly, or misunderstood as an "agenda."

△ Are you ready to play along by answering a few questions in the name of empowering you some more in the classroom? Let's do this!

Okay, first question:
Of the two topics below, which one piques your interest more? △

1. Colonial history
2. Colonial history from the perspective of the colonized

I hear you saying "Hmm, seems like #2 because it adds a bit of a twist." Fabulous. Next, have a look at these sentences:

1. Research methods is the process for developing knowledge.
2. Research methods is the process of developing knowledge—*and*— discussing how subjectivity is built into that knowledge.

Which of these sentences causes questions to pop into your head? You might have questions about both! But if you had to choose one that makes you pause and say "Hmm, wait . . . what?," which one does that? Of course, there's no right or wrong here, but take a moment to note your answer. Was it #1 or #2? Now here's a final pair of phrases for you to ponder. What if I said let's examine:

1. US racial and ethnic groups—or—
2. US racial and ethnic groups in their own right, not only in comparison to whites

What comes to mind in this case? I wonder whether you're asking "How are these different?" Or maybe you have a bunch of questions that crop up in a rapid-fire manner? If so, you're definitely not alone. Take a moment to note which of these two inspires more interest in you, #1 or #2?

Now let me ask you a final question before we dive into some practical tools you can use. As academics we spend so much time in our heads focusing on ideas. For a change, I'm asking you a question about your feelings:

Did you read any of the items in the pairs above and feel an emphatic YES? Perhaps you felt curiosity? Surprise? Confusion? Or any ol' feeling in your gut?

Take a moment to notice that feeling. △

Excellence of WFOC's Teaching:
Shaking It Up Is the Right Thing to Do

In this chapter, we are celebrating the natural way you and women faculty of color include diverse and multiple points of view in the classroom. You do it as a matter of course, because you yourself are one of those diverse viewpoints, and well, you can't help it! But there's more to it than that.

There's a very specific technique at play here in each of the pairings I've posed above. And surprise! You use this technique All. The. Time. You're doing it excellently—sometimes intentionally, other times intuitively, and still other times because you know you're supposed to. Great job!

More good news: This teaching technique of including multiple and diverse perspectives is supported—robustly—by the SoTL. You're doing it already, you're doing it well and . . . there's evidence to back you up. Good, right? Well, the twist is that even though doing this encourages thinking, motivates additional learning, asking questions; and conjures up the emotions—affirmation, curiosity, confusion—all necessary for learning, some people are going to try to stop you from doing it, and even punish you. It's infuriating really, but it's the truth. So, what can you do to thrive in spite of this threat to your diverse perspectives (and career)?

Look, integrating diverse perspectives into your curriculum is a very effective teaching technique that women faculty of color use more than other faculty. Don't let people stop you from using it. Let's give you all you need to clap back at those naysayers.

Here I go again with some more questions for you. If you think you can hear me chuckling, you would be right! I am a teacher and writer who loves questions.

These are the questions I have for you:

> In your view, is student learning at its best when *all the information is the same?*
> What about when *all the content is coming from the same perspective?* Will excellent learning take place?

If you said absolutely not, you're of course correct. There's so much SoTL research that supports the practice of teaching diverse and multiple perspectives. And that research makes it clear that everyone should be doing what you're doing in classes as this practice improves student learning, improves cognitive complexity, etc.

Teaching diverse (i.e., multiple) perspectives is EXACTLY what you should be doing in the classroom. You need to shake it up a little bit for students to aid their learning. For example, imagine scenario one, where students learn about racial and ethnic minority groups in the United States. They would probably soak up new information about each group's facts, figures, and sociocultural history in comparison to whites. Even a pretty straightforward delivery is bound to be intriguing due to the forbidden information being revealed in this US context that shuns talking about race. A teaching win, right? Well . . . not so fast.

By contrast imagine instead a second scenario where students learn about racial and ethnic minority groups. But this time, instead of only teaching it the regular way where groups get compared to whites, you also teach about each group in their own right. You are explicit with students how a comparative lens defines White as the "norm" and thus racial and ethnic groups as deficient. As their invisible "deficiency" goggles begin to fall, students may ask a million previously unconsidered questions. To offset this taken-for-granted "normal/abnormal" lens when teaching this topic, you include scholarship from marginalized groups' perspectives that highlights these groups' nuances and strengths. Students may begin to challenge previously gained knowledge about these groups as they incorporate this new knowledge and, more significantly—begin to shift them toward a fuller understanding of this topic.

Picture the student discussions in both of these scenarios—which might produce a more active student discussion rather than a passive acceptance of knowledge? Can you envision how revealing a hidden lens or adding an additional lens can encourage a deeper consideration of this topic for students?

The first scenario is an example of race and ethnic relations taught narrowly, and while learning seems to occur, it wouldn't really push students to grow and learn more deeply. In contrast, the second scenario adds a diverse lens, adds a different perspective, adds a non-mainstream perspective, and it's this breadth of approach to a topic that can improve student learning. The second scenario shakes things up.

The Evidence-Based Benefits of the Diverse and Multiple Perspectives You Teach Are Plentiful

Are you beginning to have a clearer idea of what this teaching technique of adding diverse and multiple perspectives does for student learning? To support you in connecting your classroom work with data, here's a list of the evidence-based benefits that you can refer to when needed.

Teaching that is inclusive of multiple, diverse, and non-mainstream perspectives results in many improvements in students,[1] such as:

- Improves cognitive skills
- Improves critical thinking
- Helps students enter adulthood (e.g., workplaces) better prepared for diversity
- Prepares students for citizenship
- Increases creativity
- Increases confidence and safety with differences later in life
- Increases open-mindedness
- Provides a more comprehensive understanding of course goals
- Provides a more comprehensive understanding of people
- Increases empathy
- Generates ideas of higher quality
- Generates ideas of higher feasibility
- Generates ideas of higher effectiveness
- Stimulates a higher level of critical analysis of decisions and alternatives

- Produces greatest engagement in active thinking
- Produces growth in intellectual engagement
- Produces growth in intellectual motivation
- Produces growth in intellectual skills
- Produces growth in academic skills
- Fosters cognitive growth
- Fosters personal growth (including cultural knowledge and understanding, leadership abilities, and commitment to promoting understanding)
- Develops more accurate knowledge
- Teaches students to think more deeply, actively, and critically when confronted with biases and erroneous information
- Decreases prejudice
- Increases cognitive development
- Increases civic behaviors and dispositions

By contrast, when diverse and multiple perspectives are not taught, student learning is constrained and reduced. Narrow, mainstream-only perspectives reduce student learning, period, end of story.

Threat:
"They" Don't Get It and That's Not Required

People who don't get it will likely be surprised to read the scenarios below, which are a painfully common, sometimes daily burden if you're a woman of color academic. The challenges are many, incessant, and too often invisible or ignored. While ultimately it doesn't matter whether people understand the challenges because you can have a thriving academic career regardless, it's definitely helpful when people make an effort. To that end, right here in the broad daylight of this chapter here are just a smattering of real-life examples from women of color's classrooms. I bet you have some experiences you can add!

THEY DON'T "GET IT" (AND THAT'S NOT REQUIRED) 91

- "Three white students wrote letters to the director of my program stating that I was biased and that I did not support them."
- "I've literally been called racist in my evals (though not sexist or classist, even though I cover those issues, too). My student evals almost tanked my tenure at my prior institution."
- "I am often critiqued for being racist or focusing on race too much. It got so bad at my last institution, I had to add information in my syllabus about 'productive discomfort' and heavily emphasize that all of my lectures are based on research. (FYI, these two moves were in response to my colleagues as well, not just students.)"
- "The biggest issues have been getting them over their discomfort with the material and getting them to see the world differently."

As you contemplated these scenarios, did your inner voice say . . . "Yup, I've experienced that" or "Uh . . . hello I'm experiencing that RIGHT NOW!" In fact, research tells us that many women of color faculty are in the same boat. So you're being challenged for teaching diverse and multiple perspectives? For teaching content that's not considered to be mainstream? Here's what I want to tell you right now . . . FORGET those challengers!

You know good and well that the content you're teaching is scholarship but I want to encourage you to think about exactly WHY you're including and teaching that diverse perspectives content. Might it be:

You're including it because it's your research area?
You're including it because it's your disciplinary training?
You're including it because it's your specialty?

These are 100 percent legitimate reasons to proceed with these diverse and multiple perspectives teaching intact. Unfortunately, a lot of times folks challenge women faculty of color, saying "Oh that's just your opinion" or "You're biased" or "You have an agenda." Heck no, you don't have an agenda! If you did, it'd be the same agenda those challengers have: To teach to your scholarship, your expertise, your academic training. That does not mean that it's your opinion, however. It means that it's your expertise, just like every other faculty member is in the classroom teaching their expertise.

Heck No, There's No Agenda Behind the Teaching! It's Just Not "Mainstream"

This pushback to claims of having an agenda is not a new struggle for women faculty of color, in fact this kind of pushback is longstanding. In just one example, bell hooks describes the challenges she and Chandra Talpade Mohanty had as scholars in making the "agenda" of their mainstream colleagues visible:

> Emphasizing that—*a white male professor in an English department who teaches only work by "great white men" is making a political decision*—we had to work consistently against and through the overwhelming *will on the part of folks to deny the politics of* racism, sexism, heterosexism, and so forth that inform how and what we teach.
>
> We found again and again that almost everyone, especially the old guard, were more disturbed by the overt recognition of the role our political perspectives play in shaping pedagogy than by *their passive acceptance of ways of teaching and learning that reflect biases, particularly a white supremacist standpoint.* [emphasis added][2]

Similar to hooks and Mohanty, you're being challenged because your teaching content is not mainstream. You could say that their curriculum revealing the bias of white male professors was a little outside the dominant narrative! Well, what you teach—whatever your discipline, and whatever courses you're carrying this semester—is your version of this. You're being challenged because what you have in your course represents perspectives that have been excluded, and by including them you're a threat to the status quo.

In short, I hope you will carry forward zero doubt about this, and instead proceed with greater groundedness in your step. There's nothing wrong with the content you're including. When the naysayers arrive, take a page from hooks and Mohanty and give them the proverbial middle finger inside your mind.

Now I know that's easier said than done when you're being challenged by people who think that they know what is legitimate knowledge. Or they think that they know what's legitimate teaching content, which to me is legitimately laughable. Whoever hired you did so because you have a particular specialty but then when they see what that looks like up close, all of a sudden they've decided that is just your opinion versus your actual expertise. Nope.

I'm going to make sure you have what you need to make it plain in your teaching materials, in the verbal and written narratives that you're having with folks about the diverse and multiple-perspective content you're including, why you're doing it that way, how it's not an agenda of some kind, and of course we're going to use the SoTL to do that.

Strategic Action:
Enforce Their Embrace of Your Critical Theory Genius

Having established how beneficial multiple perspectives are, what is up with the resistance so many women faculty of color encounter? Here's the thing, neither your colleagues nor your students know a thing about the research that supports this. They're simply doing what they know, which is seeing the world through their particular focused and usually narrow lens. Anyone who is attached to their lens will be challenged by some of the things you teach. In fact, it may very well challenge their sense of self, make their knowledge feel illegitimate, or even cause them to doubt their many years of work.

On the other hand, white faculty may feel that they *are already sharing multiple perspectives*. But often they're sharing multiple perspectives from essentially the same dominant viewpoint and that's confronting for them. For example, they might teach:

> Perspective A1 (e.g., white French elite/colonizer) and Perspective A2 (e.g., white British elite/colonizer) in a course and consider that to be multiple perspectives.

But here in this book, we're talking about a much broader spectrum of perspectives, including those of women of color faculty. And these are not just variations of perspective A. No, instead, truly diverse teaching content might include:

Perspective A (e.g., white elite/colonizer) as well as perspective B (e.g., colonized people of color).

When you teach diverse and multiple perspectives such as these, given the resistance you'll likely face, make sure others are aware of their numerous benefits.

> **For example, your conversations with colleagues and your submitted review materials might say something like this:**
>
> Research demonstrates that my inclusion of a broader than traditional set of perspectives in the scholarship I teach has many benefits for student learning such as increases in _____ (insert the evidence-based benefits of diverse perspectives listed in this chapter you think apply; e.g., cognitive skills, critical thinking, and preparation for workplace diversity).

Or maybe an empowered faculty member might be courageous and not teach perspective A at all and instead challenge students to learn even further through:

Perspective B (e.g., colonized people of color) plus perspective C (e.g., the intersection of race and gender), perspective D (e.g., sexual orientation), and perspective E (e.g., external criticizer of the white elite/colonizer).

Okay that last example was a lot, and that kind of teaching is a lot of work that can go unrecognized and be discouraged, but it is of immeasurable value when it comes to learning outcomes as research shows. So you must ACT to ensure that the value you provide is recognized in informal colleague conversations and in formal reviews.

> **Your insistence that they recognize the value your teaching adds might be a few sentences such as this in your review materials:**
>
> There is great value in my teaching of scholarship that lies outside of the traditional "canon." Namely, the diverse perspectives of my teaching content produce more _____ in student learning outcomes.
>
> (insert the evidence-based benefits of diverse perspectives listed in this chapter you think apply; e.g., comprehensive understanding of course goals, open-mindedness, active thinking, accurate knowledge, etc.).

What I've just described above is the fact that we as women faculty of color—sometimes without even realizing it—apply a critical lens to our scholarship[3]. And this is what produces perspectives other than the dominant "A" perspective (e.g., white male colonizer.). A critical lens is an approach that focuses on reflection and critique in order to reveal and challenge power structures.[4] So our approach to scholarship and thus teaching is that we don't always accept knowledge as taken for granted. We ask questions, we turn it over and upside down like we'd examine a rock in our hand.

In turn, that examination identifies challengeable assumptions and power dynamics. From there, we insert ideas and voices and lenses that have been excluded, silenced, imagined, and overlooked, such as our own as women of color. The scholarship doesn't have to be about race or diversity . . . if you're overturning long-held assumptions, if you're questioning the dominant viewpoint on whatever the topic is. . . . you are shaking things up. That's what you're doing naturally, that's the way that you approach the work.

And that's essentially your superpower, right? The genius of what you're doing is applying a critical perspective to the scholarship you both create and teach[5]. And you must make this superpower and its benefits clear in your conversations with peers and in reviews to protect your classroom and career.

Threat:

Name the Resistance to Your Diverse Perspectives

Through working with women faculty of color for decades, I know the resistance to something as simple as diverse viewpoints can be exhausting and demoralizing. What seems so simple—including contrary voices—just shouldn't be this hard, right? Of course, what we're really talking about is power. The person with the mainstream viewpoint wants to remain as the mainstream viewpoint but progress and change come only when those things are challenged.

For what it's worth, you're in good company as you challenge the resistance. You're following the footsteps of hooks[6] and Freire,[7] who both took a critical perspective to pedagogy. Their critical pedagogy ideas continue to rankle those who cling to the dominant "mainstream" ways of teaching even today. The same way that the critical scholarship you teach rankles those who cling to dominant "mainstream" ideas about what is "legitimate" in your field. Let's take a closer look at that resistance.

Remember the examples we opened this chapter with? Perhaps you're teaching colonial history or literature or philosophy or whatever—but doing so from the perspective of the colonized racial minorities. Or your content doesn't have anything to do with race or diversity at all. In a research methods course, you might be teaching knowledge as human and subjective rather than as objective and disconnected from humans. You could be inserting excluded voices or contributors into the history of the development of a theoretical construct, scientific discovery, etc. For example, you might teach about mathematician Katherine Johnson's previously erased but prominent role in the launch of the first human flight to the moon.

THEY DON'T "GET IT" (AND THAT'S NOT REQUIRED)   97

Teaching any of the above or similar may cause strong and visceral responses in those who are tightly bound to the dominant or mainstream perspective that you are displacing. These are the folks who have invested their being, their scholarship, their experiences, everything in their classrooms—into this thing that you are flipping upside down. Suffice to say, they may respond strongly and aggressively not realizing that you're not engaging with their work with ill will. You do so as part of your critical lens, a long-standing and much-honored approach embraced by many. Regrettably, there are consequences for those that do so—especially when you hold marginalized statuses.

Here are a couple of different ways to view people's reaction to your critical lens—to the scholarship you teach.

Cognitive Dissonance

Cognitive dissonance occurs when an individual is introduced to a new belief they perceive as clashing or inconsistent with their current ones. In this case, your colleagues have established and long-held ideas that your knowledge doesn't fit with. Enter cognitive dissonance with a vengeance. Some of your colleagues may be fine with this. But others may reject and diminish your ideas as their way of removing that stress. This person in your life is saying "That can't be true otherwise I've been living a lie."

Take, for example, the people who believed the Earth was flat, assuming that you're not one of them! They were so bought into this belief that proof of Earth's roundness was unacceptable to them. The dissonance was too great for them so they rejected the possibility of a non-flat Earth.

Refusal to Think Critically

> Critical thinking requires discernment ... It is a way of approaching ideas that aims to understand core, underlying truths, not simply the superficial truth that may be most obviously visible ... keeping an open mind is an essential requirement to critical thinking.[8]

We often talk about students as refusing to think critically in our classrooms. But this is something that our colleagues are not exempt from either. When we teach content that puts their worldview into context as *one* worldview, not THE worldview, chaos breaks loose in their gray matter.

Critical thinking is a skill that must be developed and is not used universally. In other words, we have to work at keeping our minds open to dissenting views, and we naturally pick and choose which things we'll think critically about.

Some examples of how a refusal to think critically can show up in students *and colleagues* are below. Take a moment to see which ones you're most familiar with, and ask which ones you've experienced recently.

- Inflexible or rigid thinking
- Intolerance of divergent or conflicting views
- Unwillingness to treat all viewpoints as equally valid before taking a closer look
- Attachment to one's own beliefs
- No consideration of points of view other than one's own
- No consideration of points of view that do not benefit themselves
- Rejection of criticism and constructive feedback
- Does not amend existing knowledge in light of new ideas and experiences
- Does not explore new, alternative, or "unusual" ideas

While this list can be confronting, it is real, and data show that only 10–15 percent of women faculty of color feel their teaching is supported by colleagues. Data also show that students are more likely to behave aggressively towards and give low ratings to women faculty of color. But you don't need me to tell you that, do you? Because all you need is to read your most recent teaching review or show up in the classroom to experience it firsthand. Barriers to critical thinking[9]—for example, the close-mindedness list above—can look suspiciously similar to student and colleague refusals of ideas, specifically to the diverse scholarship you teach.

Imagine for a moment a colleague's intolerance of teaching colonial history from the perspective of the colonized racial minority? How about one who can't detach from their own biases to consider the creation of knowledge as subjective? Or colleagues who won't amend their "stories" about who developed or originated concepts, innovations, historical moments—even in light of new knowledge, ideas, or experiences? This is the world in which we're living, and why we must equip ourselves to thrive despite these pressures.

The Power to Silence and Punish Diverse Perspectives

The thing about dissonance and a refusal to think critically is that—while problematic—both can still be all fine and well when those involved have equal standing. But as women faculty of color—*we know it's often not all fine and well* because we don't have equal standing given our marginalized statuses. So when we teach a differing perspective, and those with dominant statuses holding the dominant or mainstream perspective refuse to think critically, or they experience dissonance, we often end up getting punished for that. Students and colleagues who are invested in the mainstream or "taken for granted" perspectives are in a position of power and have the means to create harm toward you. Poor student evaluations or tenure reviews of teaching are just two examples. In this scenario you aren't on equal footing; the power dynamic is unequal.

Now you might be wondering what I mean by power dynamic. If we go back to the flat earth believers for a moment, it's as if these individuals were the most powerful people at the time, and they used that power to pass judgment on critical thinkers who proved that the Earth is round. Even though one of these ideas isn't more powerful than the other, if the flat earthers were in power, they could (and some did) punish, ridicule, and even jail the critical thinkers. That is the power dynamic at play.

When it comes to your teaching, I want to make it plain that we are entering a conversation that has existed for a very long time. And that conversation states: You are experiencing resistance or attempts to silence the scholarship you teach because they're not the ideas of the powerful; they aren't the ideas that justify or maintain the status quo. Point blank. This is not a new idea; it's not only happening to you; it's existed for centuries.

The familiar, recent and mainstream proponents of these ideas are Marx and Engels who in 1845 wrote:

> The ideas of the ruling class are in every epoch the ruling ideas . . . The ruling ideas are nothing more than the ideal expression of the dominant material relationships grasped as ideas.[10]

And guess who is tasked with this gatekeeping? Who maintains the dominant group's ideas as the main ideas? Intellectuals! While faculty like to present and think of themselves as objective, according to Gramsci,[11] intellectuals actively teach and encourage folks to adopt the dominant group's ideas.

So it's not that your colleagues who are resisting your diverse course content are outwardly saying, "We're dominant, we're privileged, that's why our voice should be the only or loudest one." They're doing quite the opposite. They're trying to make their views seem like they're the normal views. They shush and punish any scholarship you teach that highlights that theirs is the view of the privileged. They work to present their scholarship as "taken for granted" ideas that "everyone" agrees to. When that is done, the source and beneficiaries of those ideas become hidden. This is how they silence your views that counter the ideas of the powerful. When the ruling ideas maintained by privileged academics appear to be the "norm" (as per Gramsci's hegemony[12])—in contrast your diverse, multiple perspectives and marginalized scholarship appears subjective and abnormal.

More recently, women scholars of color such as Patricia Hill Collins[13] expressed her similar belief that "dominant thought (is) reflective of power narratives." Her work expressly aims to introduce other narratives as a result. You are continuing in this same tradition as her by including diverse scholarship, non-mainstream narratives, and multiple perspectives in your classroom content.

What Resistance Might Look Like in Real Life: The Case of Adjunct Vasquez and Professor Smith

Let's take the example of Adjunct Vasquez. In her field, she takes a stand for including the silenced voices of women of color, and her resulting experience with colleagues is that of continual resistance (dissonance, lack of critical thinking, or silencing), which in turns leads to them devaluing and discounting the scholarship in her teaching, research, service, and more. This is in comparison to white male Professor Smith in the same department who has been teaching the ideas that have been popular for over 50 years. Which professor would you surmise has less student and colleague resistance to their teaching content? Has less trouble in teaching and other reviews? Gets ahead, tenured, and promoted more easily?

Regardless of whether your dominant status colleagues realize this is what they're doing or not, their scholarship and lived experiences often represent the dominant ideas in your field. These powerful folks will continue to behave in ways that silence non-dominant ideas. And the powerful have ways to punish you for your non-dominant perspectives—namely in reviews. So whether you know it or not, your non-dominant ideas are being silenced, a little or a lot. Challenges to the diverse and multiple perspectives scholarship you teach as legitimate is not a neutral, objective, race or gender-free activity. Quite the contrary—most often these challenges to your legitimacy are power trying to assert itself. And this will have negative consequences for your retention, tenure, and promotion reviews so you must both identify (i.e., name the resistance) and act to offset this threat to you and your career.

You might be thinking "Yikes, does this mean my colleagues are elitist, sexist, and racist?" While that may or may not be true, the point is that this is generally how higher education works. This is a commentary about how power operates. What I want most for you is to have a refreshed understanding of student and colleague resistance to your diverse teaching content. Rather than tell a story of you and your teaching as less than or illegitimate, or not scholarly, what's needed is an objective retelling. Your teaching and you are vulnerable in reviews on a systemic level, and seeing it with clear eyes helps you to triumph and thrive in spite of these things. In spite of the self-interested, hidden, and powerful narrative that is trying to convince you and others otherwise, there is nothing wrong with the diverse and multiple-perspectives scholarship that you are teaching. And in fact, you should be rewarded in reviews for the benefits your diverse teaching content provides to the students, university, and society at large.

SoTL Minefield:
The Scholarship of Teaching and Learning Does and Does Not Have Your Back

As someone who has spent many years on the journey to empower fellow diverse faculty to teach effectively and thrive in their careers, I hope you're inspired—even a little—to use data from the SoTL to back up your teaching. All of your fabulous diverse, inclusive, and non-mainstream perspectives have solid data-driven arguments behind them. The SoTL is the main body of literature you can lean on, yet I have to add a cautionary note. It's important that you understand—the SoTL also does *not* have your back.

While the SoTL says "Oh, this is the way to do it—include diverse perspectives and voices, it has all these gains, this is the teaching strategy everyone should be using"—it often doesn't acknowledge the consequences of doing so when you're a woman faculty of color. Stated another way, the SoTL doesn't acknowledge the difference between teaching marginalized perspectives as a white person, and teaching marginalized perspectives as a marginalized individual. A woman of color teaching white students about content that is marginalized is very different from a white person teaching white students contrarian content.

The SoTL folks know that teaching diverse content is going to improve student learning and encourages *everyone* to do so, but they *don't* acknowledge that you do so at a cost when you're a woman of color faculty. They don't take into account that we embody and occupy statuses that have less power—in society and in higher education. This is a huge overlooked hole within this body of work.

I suspect the assumption is that we will be treated like faculty with powerful statuses—that we'll be rewarded, recognized, and published for "innovative" teaching content. But for us women of color it more often looks something like this:

> Rather than being acknowledged for bringing more diverse voices and my experience to the classroom, I was told (and sometimes inferred) "I wasn't appropriate," or the lesson wasn't "appropriate," or nothing was said to me at all, and I would get a check-in call from my associate dean at the time or the provost for a meeting about teaching and learning.

Let's be clear—as the above research quote illustrates—colleagues are silencing your diverse voices and perspectives, calling your teaching illegitimate, essentially punishing you for teaching it. And this is more nefarious than disgruntled students and colleagues who are also punishing you in tenure reviews as another woman of color research participant shared:

> "I've literally been called racist in my evals (though not sexist or classist, even though I cover those issues, too). My student evals almost tanked my tenure at my prior institution."

When we teach diverse or non-mainstream content, we have to navigate or swim upstream against the unequal power dynamics of student and colleague resistance. And as if the stress of that constant battling wasn't enough, we have to be ready to fend off the threats those nagging but powerful naysayers pose to our tenure reviews. Because if we didn't battle and stay ready—we'd be out of a job. All for using an evidence-based teaching practice.

So the SoTL absolutely gets it right by providing all the research evidence that teaching diverse perspectives is important to do. In that way—SoTL scholars have your back. But they don't acknowledge that women faculty of color who engage in this particular strategy may experience negative consequences—especially in their high stakes reviews. This is a problem that I work on with women faculty of color at every level—how to be empowered and thrive when confronted with vulnerable scenarios so your academic career isn't sacrificed to these threats.

Strategic Action:

Harvest Rewards for Your Contributions to Campus Goals

We've covered a lot of ground, and there's already a lot you can shift about how you consider and engage in the work of teaching in this chapter. In just a couple of paragraphs I have a summary of key points for you, along with some actions you can take this week. But before we go there, I'd like to give you something. I want you to listen closely because I'm only going to say this once. Just kidding. I'm going to say it a million times and with a big smile on my face.

What I want to give you is credit for your labor. By including diverse perspectives, you are doing something that is fundamental to the existence of your institution. All those stated mission, vision, and accreditation goals that your university has posted on its website, in brochures, and on banners? *You're the faculty member that's fulfilling those promises.* All of the language used about teaching students how to function in the real world? *You're the faculty member who's providing that.* Oh, the institution wants its students to know how to interact across differences, how to understand complex problems, how to, you know what . . . just fill in the blank, whatever. All of the things that your institution says about "understanding communities?" Just look at the goals on your campus that relate to the benefits of diverse and multiple perspectives. Guess who is doing that? You, you, you, and YOU.[14]

So when your colleagues are resisting you teaching diverse content—in addition to pointing them back to the scholarship on teaching and learning and that very long list of benefits of this

THEY DON'T "GET IT" (AND THAT'S NOT REQUIRED)   105

teaching strategy above? I need you to point back to the very goals that are stated on your university's website, your department's website, your unit's website. I'm pretty sure there is something there that has to do with a global economy, democratic citizenship, intellectual inquiry, societal contributions, etc. Don't believe me? Go ahead and take a look around. I'll wait. [Smile.] Once you've pinpointed those statements, harvest the rewards for fulfilling those promises. Grab ALL of the rewards. While mission statements can and do change, below are a few illustrations. Though keep in mind, the real power is in identifying the goals on your campus that apply to your teaching.

First, you might be surprised to see these goals in the mission statements of large state universities:

- Florida State University [...] strives to instill the strength, skill, and character essential for *lifelong learning, personal responsibility, and sustained achievement* within a community that fosters free inquiry. [emphasis added][15]
- [The University of Iowa] provides exceptional teaching and transformative educational experiences that *prepare students for success and fulfillment in an increasingly diverse and global environment*; advances scholarly and creative endeavor through leading-edge research and artistic production; and *brings learning and discovery into the service of the people of the state of Iowa, the nation, and the world, improving lives through education, health care, arts and culture, and community and economic vitality.* [emphasis added][16]

Here are the goals in the mission statement of a private liberal arts college:

- The purpose of a Bowdoin education—the mission of the College—is therefore to *assist a student to deepen and broaden intellectual capacities* that are also attributes of maturity and wisdom: self-knowledge, intellectual honesty, clarity of thought, depth of knowledge, an independent capacity to learn, mental courage, self-discipline, *tolerance of and interest in differences of culture and belief,* and a *willingness to serve the common good* and subordinate self to higher goals. [emphasis added][17]

And this is what relevant goals look like in the mission statement of a university focused primarily on STEM fields:

- MIT is dedicated to providing its students with an education that combines rigorous academic study and the excitement of discovery with the support and *intellectual stimulation of a diverse campus community*. We seek to *develop in each member of the MIT community the ability and passion to work wisely, creatively, and effectively for the betterment of humankind*. [emphasis added][18]

Finally, these goals are still illustrated in the mission of this university that has faced many legal challenges to diversity in higher education:

- UCLA's primary purpose as a public research university is *the creation, dissemination, preservation and application of knowledge for the betterment of our global society*. To fulfill this mission, UCLA is committed to academic freedom in its fullest terms: We value open access to information, *free and lively debate conducted with mutual respect for individuals, and freedom from intolerance*. In all of our pursuits, *we strive for excellence and diversity, recognizing that openness and inclusion produce true quality*. These values underlie our three institutional responsibilities: education, research and public service. [emphasis added][19]

You see what I'm saying, I'm sure. *By teaching diverse and multiple perspectives, you're clearly promoting all of these campus goals!* And no one else is doing more to support these institutional missions. Current context posing explicit threats to these types of goals? Read this endnote.[20]

One additional thing you're doing when you include diverse and multiple perspectives is helping to retain diverse students. When diverse students can see themselves in what you teach, you increase the relevancy of the content for them, you increase their identity as a student and as a knowledge producer, and all of these wonderful outcomes increase diverse students' sense of belonging and retention.[21]

Long story short, take time to make all this institutional service you provide explicit in the materials you submit when you're being reviewed for teaching and in your conversations with colleagues about teaching. It's your opportunity to harvest the rewards of the value your teaching brings to the university's proclaimed goals.

Reaping those rewards might be reflected in a few statements such as:

The diverse/multiple perspectives in the scholarship I teach aids the university in reaching its explicitly stated goals. Specifically, my teaching content produces increased _____ (insert the diverse perspective outcomes that align with your campus' mission statement) in students.

And these contribute directly to the university's goal(s) of _____ (insert the mission outcomes that align with your diverse perspective outcomes) found in its mission statement: (Include the mission statement and italicize the parts that your teaching content provide for the university).

An illustration:

The diverse/multiple perspectives in the scholarship I teach aids the university in reaching its explicitly stated goals. Specifically, my teaching content produces increased *intellectual and academic skills, leadership abilities, and intellectual motivation* in students. And these contribute directly to furthering the university's goals of *strength, skill, and character for lifelong learning, personal responsibility, and sustained achievement* found in its mission:

> Florida State University . . . strives to *instill the strength, skill, and character essential for lifelong learning, personal responsibility, and sustained achievement* within a community that fosters free inquiry. [emphasis added]

(continued)

> Additionally the scholarship I teach provides service to the university as research demonstrates these additional scholarly perspectives greatly aid in supporting the "Dynamic Environment," "Engaged Community," and "Inspired Excellence" as described in FSU's Core Values. [I just added this sentence in for good measure! Ha!]

You don't need anybody's permission to teach what you know is right. If you only knew it in your gut before reading this chapter, now you know that what you're doing is right from the SoTL perspective and from the perspective of helping a university meet its stated goals. Don't entertain inappropriate questions or comments about whether or not your scholarship is legitimate. Some people just don't get it and it's okay to ignore 'em. Onward!

Summary

I know I shared a lot in this chapter, but that's because it's one of the most actionable topics in the book. I hope you take that action encouraged by the prompts below and find your teaching easier, more defendable, and greatly rewarded in reviews. Here are the main takeaways I want you to remember above all else:

- You are a teaching genius. Whether you knew it or didn't—the content you and WFOC naturally teach in the classroom is to be celebrated. So, stick your chest out and be proud.
- Students and colleagues are going to resist you and WFOC teaching diverse or multiple-perspectives course content. Know what that resistance looks like so that you can effectively put it in its place—off your list of things to worry about.
- Shake off haters by becoming intimately familiar with the list of benefits to teaching diverse or multiple perspectives. Readily flaunt the list to anyone who needs reminding— how you teach is backed by data.
- The resistance you experience to your diverse content is about power and power dynamics. Period. Don't be afraid to just call it what it is.

- SoTL doesn't warn of nor acknowledge the specific risks to WFOC for engaging in the excellence practice of teaching diverse or multiple perspectives.
- The diverse perspectives that you and WFOC teach adds up to a lot of unacknowledged service work helping your campus meet its stated goals. Claim your labor and its benefits. If you're going to get hated on for it, absolutely get credit for the work you're doing to fulfill the university's mission in your retention/promotion/tenure reviews.

Empowering Actions You Can Take This Week

In each chapter of this book, I aim to cover one distinct challenge to women faculty of color, and to answer that, provide at least one evidence-based strategic teaching practice. The problem is, these are irrelevant if you don't do anything with them. So finish off this chapter by engaging with the actions below, which will help get you ready to enact this chapter's strategic action. And make sure you work on these with a fellow WFOC faculty member or join the community of Empowered readers to discuss.

1. What ideas in this chapter really sunk in? validated and affirmed you and your teaching?
2. Which of these small actions will you take after reading this chapter?
   a. Look at your own campus' mission (or diversity) statement and note how you help fulfill your campus' goals.
   b. Draft one sentence that describes the student gains produced by you teaching diverse or multiple perspectives.
   c. Draft one sentence that describes how your critical lens shakes up the mainstream perspective on your course topic.
   d. Add the above two sentences to (1) your teaching materials for review and (2) casual conversation with colleagues about your teaching and (3) the

learning objectives and pedagogy sections on your syllabus which you'll discuss with students throughout the course.
    e. If you're not sure how to write the above sentences or how to include them in the ways suggested above, please feel free to reach out to me at www.empoweredacademic.org.
3. Do you still struggle with feeling empowered in the face of challenges to the diverse or multiple perspectives you teach? Sign up to my email list at www.empoweredacademic.org, where I share more tips and strategies.

Pat yourself on the back for all the wonderful benefits you bring to the university and world. Then toot your horn about all of that teaching excellence in your retention, tenure and promotion review materials. Continue on to Chapter 5 to discover how your teaching methods can be more enjoyable, less fraught by pushback, and heralded in your reviews.

Chapter 5

REMAIN AUTHENTIC (AND INNOVATIVE)

Receive accolades for your teaching methods and assignments!

Discover your authentic teaching brilliance and fend off colleague and student resistance to what you do in your classroom.

△ *After some time on any given campus, you will no doubt hear a story or two like this one:*

Professor John White is an innovative teacher. Faculty colleagues and students herald him as ahead of his time, a maverick, a trendsetter, and an early adopter. The descriptors of Professor White and his innovative teaching are positive; he's an asset to the campus and is rewarded accordingly for taking teaching risks.

Students assume that the risks he takes when teaching them are worthwhile for their learning. And colleagues see his risk-taking in the classroom as indicative of his bravery and courage.

Overall, it's everyone's firm belief that John is doing the right thing in his classroom—and that is reflected in his successful retention/tenure/promotion reviews. In short, he is celebrated as a teaching hero!

In the story above—a reflection of reality on campuses around the globe—teaching innovation is good, rewarded, and welcomed. These living examples might lead you to believe that all teachers should be doing their version of Professor John White, or "Dead Poets Society" teaching, right?

Yes! Innovative teaching is often seen as a proven path to student learning, teacher accolades, and collegial praise.

Cue the record scratch.

While the positive stories of teaching are often out front, there is a much more common scenario taking place—one that is less known. The scenario often looks like this:

Professor Michelle Jones is an innovative teacher. Faculty colleagues and students view her as an outsider, a negative influence, unsubstantiated in her teaching, and untrustworthy. The descriptors of Professor Jones and her innovative teaching are negative; she is an unwelcome agitator, and is criticized and penalized for taking teaching risks.

Students and her faculty peers judge her teaching to be high-risk and worst-case scenario teaching. Students don't hesitate to criticize her teaching choices, her motivation, and even her character—commenting that she is biased and her teaching ungrounded. As for rewards? No rewards for teaching innovation here.

Overall, it's everyone's firm belief that Professor Jones is doing everything wrong in the classroom—she is vilified, and labeled a teaching failure in her unsuccessful retention/tenure/promotion reviews.

In this second story, do you believe that teaching innovation is bad, punished, and rejected in the classroom and in reviews? Or would you instead believe that Dr. Jones is a horrible teacher?

Unfortunately, the latter is what many people think. And they would be wrong. △

Professor White, a white man, and Professor Jones, a Black woman, are both engaging in teaching innovation. In fact, they're engaging in the same teaching and assessment strategies—that is to say, specifications grading using the same techniques and parameters. Yet because Dr. Jones is a Black woman, her teaching innovation isn't guarded by the force field that ensures Professor White's innovation is heralded. Of course, teaching innovation requires risk and vulnerability from them both, but because Dr. Jones is under attack for her minoritized gender and racial statuses, students and colleagues don't see her teaching innovation as best practice—they see her teaching innovation through a different lens. All this while both faculty are doing the same things.

Look—you may be facing bullying from students, pressure from colleagues, and negative teaching evaluations.[1] Any of these things are understandable reasons for you to abandon your efforts at teaching innovation. But women of color, hold tight. Your teaching does not warrant the resistance and punishment you experience. In fact, I'll say it again as I have in prior chapters . . . you are actually doing teaching RIGHT! I'm going to show you:

1. how what you do is teaching innovation (even if you don't currently think so)
2. that your teaching innovation is supported by the SoTL, and

3. how to make it plain that your authentic teaching is the WALK (not just the talk) that serves your university's mission.

This chapter gives you the antidote to the poisonous barbs thrown by students and colleagues who resist anything they're not used to. After soaking up information on teaching innovation and the SoTL, you will feel empowered to stay the course of your unique teaching gifts, and to oppose any punishment that threatens your academic career. The cherry on top? Make sure you read until the very end to learn how to be recognized and rewarded for your alignment with, and contribution to, your university's big-picture mission.

Excellence of WFOC's Teaching:
Authentic and Innovative Pedagogy Is What We Do

Let's keep it totally honest, decades of research and guidance[2] suggesting a variety of effective teaching practices hasn't changed the most common teaching strategy—the lecture.[3] Similarly, there is a proliferation of research on a range of assignments to help students demonstrate their learning. Has that dented the most commonly used tools? Nope, faculty relying on papers and exams are still in full bloom.

What does this mean? It's simple. Anyone who uses anything other than, or in addition to, lectures, exams, and papers—is automatically an innovative teacher. Just by going beyond the status quo, using a variety of evidence-backed practices already increases the robustness, depth, and amount of learning in the classroom. And guess what? This is exactly what women of color faculty are doing—teaching and assessing student learning with a robust range of teaching strategies.

So yes. It's just that clear and simple. YOU are an innovative teacher even if that isn't your intent or aim. You're achieving this just because you're you. I hope you claim this title with pride—and ensure others recognize it by writing about your innovation in your review materials.

Still not sure if this "innovative" teacher crown belongs to you? Fair enough. Then let me ask you two simple questions:

- Why do you teach as you do?
- Why do you give the assignments you do?

With a couple of decades of experience under my belt, I predict that I know at least some of your answers. Perhaps you had folks teach you in a way that didn't work for or reach you. You couldn't relate nor did you feel like you belonged in their classroom. Maybe the professor didn't make their teaching relevant to your real life. As a result, now that you're at the front of the room, you're very intentional about how you teach and assess because you don't want to make those same mistakes. You're trying to ensure students don't have the same horrible classroom experiences you had as a student.

Or, another scenario I have witnessed, perhaps you had a fantastic teacher who *was* able to connect with you, who taught and assessed in ways that you related to, and their teaching clearly applied to your life. Now you're trying to emulate that person.

If either of these examples is true to some degree, you are making adjustments to status quo teaching intuitively and/or guided by the research. This makes *you an innovative teacher.*

Still don't believe me? I'm very invested in you seeing yourself through a new lens because I've seen how much can change if we can get you there. So, let's take a look at the research which says women faculty of color are innovative teachers.[4] Point blank, women faculty of color are more likely than White faculty to use transformative[5] pedagogical techniques known to improve learning.[6] What specific techniques? For starters, innovative and transformative teaching and assessment doesn't necessarily mean doing something "fancy." In fact, I bet you recognize and likely use more than one of the innovative pedagogies in question, for example:

- Discussions
- Group work
- Case studies

- Interactive lecturing (simple breaks in the lecture where students participate in an activity that lets them work directly with the material)

Do you use at least one of the practices above? There you go. How about these status-quo elevating teaching and assessment techniques:

- Brainstorming
- Problem-solving
- Team-based learning
- Journals

I'm curious, do you now see a few more transformative practices you use in your teaching and assessment? At this point I hope you're giggling with glee seeing how familiar "innovative" and "transformative" pedagogies are to you. Let's keep this glee train rolling with further teaching and assessment practices identified in the research:

- Role-plays
- Think-pair-share
- Self-assessments
- Peer-assessments (student evaluations of each others' work)

See—you are an innovative teacher! Hopefully learning that nothing "fancy" or "elaborate" is required to hold this title helps you own this about yourself. Then, if we include some "fancier" items, which of these do you also employ to teach or assess?

- Experiential learning
- Field studies
- Multiple drafts of written work
- Reflective writing
- Community service as part of coursework
- Frequent quizzes
- Index card summaries/questions (e.g., exit tickets)
- Portfolios
- Clickers (e.g., polling techniques to check student understanding)

- Performances
- Demonstrations
- Cooperative learning
- Electronic quizzes with immediate feedback in class
- Using real-life problems
- Using student inquiry to drive learning
- Readings on racial and ethnic issues
- Readings on women's or gender issues
- Supplemental instruction outside of class and office hours
- Student presentations
- Rubric-based assessment
- Flipped classroom (e.g., students must read, watch, or listen to instructional content before class, while class time is used for projects, assignments, and discussions)

Whew! How's that for a roll call of likely familiar and already-in-use transformative and innovative teaching and assessment practices?! And even this isn't exhaustive or complete. I've shared a lot of practices here to increase the likelihood that you see something you recognize and can own about your teaching.

Again, for a lot of faculty, traditional lecturing and papers or exams are all they do. When you mix things up with a *variety* and *combination* of well-known teaching and assessment methods like the above—that is how teaching innovation looks when led by women of color. Transformative, diverse, and impactful to the students in front of them.

This is simply not your "usual smusual" teaching and assessment. Women faculty of color are also more likely than white peers to use active learning methods and collaborative teaching.[7] We engage students in higher order cognitive activities and diversity-related activities.[8] Furthermore, research shows that women of color dedicate more time to course preparation and advising.[9] All of this is evidence that we do more than the standard "lecture and paper or exam" teaching and assessment routine. The evidence is substantive.

All of this evidence-based classroom innovation should make you a teaching hero! Unfortunately, it is resisted, aggressively criticized, and even punished by students and colleagues.

Threat:
The Pushback and Resistance to Your Innovative Pedagogy

What drives me bonkers about all of this is that the colleagues who likely know nothing about the SoTL are the ones that are pressuring you to teach in only the "status quo" way. They're evaluating the way you're teaching in a negative manner because it isn't how *they* teach. Similarly, students resist because your teaching isn't familiar to them, not because it isn't effective. Both colleagues and students resist methods they haven't previously considered, and also any pedagogy other than you standing in front of the room lecturing. And let's be clear—there is a mountain of mistrust in the learning journey you're curating because of your vulnerable statuses as a woman of color.

It's important that you know you're not alone in this experience. What form does this resistance and punishment come in? Below are a few of the many examples. As you consider each, see if you can identify any that you've experienced in your academic career. It's important for you to remember that these things are evidence of oppression—interpersonal, institutional, and societal—and most definitely not failings on your part:[10]

- Low, mixed, or less than positive **student evaluation scores**—especially on the "overall" instructor quality item
- Negative student responses and comments on **course evaluations**—especially the words "doesn't teach" or "bad teacher"
- Formal classroom **observation reports** from colleagues with claims of "bad," "inexperienced," or "lesser" quality—particularly as descriptors for nontraditional teaching techniques
- **Informal narratives** (e.g., water cooler talk) from students and colleagues that spread gossip about complaints of "low" teaching quality—most common when the teaching practices in question differ from dominant teaching practices

- **Frequent and obstructive, threatening, or aggressive pressure** from colleagues and/or students to teach "how it's always been done" or to use "traditional" teaching methods such as passive lecturing, exams, and papers
- Social media exposure by colleagues and students to generate **public scrutiny, suspicion, and scorn** about your teaching practices—commonly when they aren't the widely accepted "sage on the stage" and five-page essay
- Any combination of the above which results in a woman faculty of color losing her job (e.g., failed retention or tenure bid) or failing to be promoted (e.g., failed promotion review) because the pushback—ungrounded as it is—is interpreted as "evidence"

I hope it's abundantly clear the resistance—to your multiple mode innovative pedagogy—we're discussing has significant, sometimes irrevocable consequences for women faculty of color and their careers. You are painted as an ineffective and horrible teacher. As if that isn't enough, this fiction becomes the de facto "negative evaluation" of your teaching, which in turn is ill-advisedly considered when it's time for renewal, tenure, or promotion. All of this because you're using teaching and assessment methods over and above the traditional lecture and exams or papers. That negative evaluation of your teaching is NOT sound for multiple reasons.[11] However, *your use of multiple methods to teach* and *multiple methods to assess* is absolutely sound, according to the scholarship of teaching and literature.[12] Your teaching, by definition, actually represents teaching excellence.

By now it may be clear why we lingered on the explicit definitions and examples of teaching innovation, the better to support you in owning that. This is because in order to head off the negative consequences of pushback from colleagues and students, we must equip you to defend your teaching innovation and excellence in your reviews. In fact, the most current dialogue in the SoTL that supports your teaching and assessment (i.e., pedagogy) innovation describes three big picture reasons to do it. Knowledge transfer, the biological basis of learning, and student engagement.[13]

Next up? Let's equip you with how to respond to naysayers so you and your academic career are better protected.

Strategic Action:
Make It Plain Your Authentic Teaching Walks the SoTL Talk

Let's check in with Professor Michelle Jones and see what's happening. Would it surprise you if I said that on a regular basis she gets pressured by colleagues to teach in the traditional ways? Like so many other women faculty of color, she's pressured to lecture, and lecture only, especially if that's how it's always been done in her particular discipline. Can you relate? Have you by chance been pressured to eliminate group projects, or eliminate assignment prompts about current events, real world issues, or topics relevant to students' lives? In essence, the culture of many departments sustains the status quo in teaching. Guess what? All of this is horrible guidance and the antithesis of effective teaching.

It's been clearly shown that the teaching innovation carried out by women faculty of color is good for students. All that remains is for you to become versed in what the SoTL says about your teaching excellence so you can present this evidence in your retention/tenure/promotion reviews.

So what does the SoTL say? Much like in prior chapters, it says definitively: You are doing it right! And we can all be rightfully joyful and proud of that. Take a moment to be proud, and maybe even bust out a laugh—simply put, using more than one strategy to teach, and using more than one strategy to assess students, is the most effective way to teach, period.

The Case for Teaching and Assessing in Multiple Ways: It Upgrades Static Knowledge to Transferable Knowledge

Take what Dr. Michelle Miller, cognitive psychologist and author of *Remembering and Forgetting in the Age of Technology: Teaching,*

Learning, and the Science of Memory in a Wired World[14] and *Minds Online: Teaching Effectively with Technology*,[15] has to say about the cognitive science of learning and in particular about the principle of knowledge transfer:

> Why not simply lecture? Why do we have to lecture for certain material? And then we stop and do a case study and then we do some other demanding activity that's maybe, you know, not closed ended (is maybe more messy). And why is that so? Cognitive psychologists have observed for a long time, this illusion of fluency, this illusion of ease, that, "hey, sitting in this lecture, it feels easy and good". But when it comes to 'can you apply this or are you really working out the skills?', you're not going to have a good sense of that. And [students and colleagues] mistake the kind of smooth, ease and fluency of taking in that information for learning and that that's not always what's happening. [Their] attitudes may reflect the commonest misconceptions about learning and memory—that memory works a little bit like a video camera, basically. So—I'm here, I'm present, I'm looking at you and breathing the air in the classroom, therefore the stuff that's sort of going on is somehow registering and in a permanent way in my brain. And nothing could be further from the truth from a memory knowledge acquisition standpoint.
>
> So . . . teaching using multiple approaches—beyond the static lecture and exam—aids in knowledge transfer. Lecture may make static knowledge available, but that's insufficient in today's classrooms. What we know about how to make knowledge usable in real life is clear, we need to imitate as closely as possible the real-world situations that the knowledge will be required in when we teach. Without this, classroom learning is learning for learning's sake. In other words, what we know is multiple choice exams aren't great, students can learn how to take multiple choice exams. Static knowledge is next to useless by next week, it's not knowledge anymore, it's

lost. Teaching in an innovative way upgrades static knowledge to retained, or transferable knowledge, knowledge that stays with the student in ways that they can use.[16]

Student learning is context-dependent so our classrooms need to imitate contexts from the real world. Savvy, evidence-based teachers don't stop with lectures. They use additional teaching and assessment strategies like stories, role plays, demonstrations, social media, hands-on assignments, etc. They use these to propel "a realistic problem into the class."[17]

That's what really engaged, really masterful teachers are doing and why it works. They're creating classroom knowledge transfer. So be sure to tell others that your teaching and assessing in multiple ways aids in knowledge transfer, and therefore teaching excellence, period.

The Case for Teaching and Assessing in Multiple Ways: Based on the Biological Basis of Learning

As we continue to explore how to ground yourself in reviews with the research on teaching innovation, let's next hear from Dr. Joshua Eyler, author of *How Humans Learn: The Science and Stories behind Effective College Teaching*[18] who says your use of multiple methods to teach and assess in the classroom is grounded in the evidence we have for how people learn most effectively:

> Our brains are not built to learn in only one way. They would be very dull brains if that were true—they'd be more like a computer, limited. As human beings, we're really built to learn from authentic engagement, by asking questions and addressing questions. So teaching strategies that are built on and rooted in inquiry are most effective.
>
> But there are also humanistic elements to this [biological basis of learning]. Teaching using stories allows for an emotional connection with the materials. An emotional connection is another biologically-based way we know

humans learn. There are lots of examples, but in short, the notion that a person or a group of students could only learn in one way pushes back against everything we know about learning. An enriched learning environment with multiple strategies can only help our students. If we were teaching someone math and all we did was continually write problems up on the board without ever giving them a chance to ask questions, try out the problem for themselves or try a similar kind of problem, we know from the literature on how people learn math that this just wouldn't work. That's like any subject. The students need to get in there, they need to have some instruction and then they need to try it out. They need classrooms that create opportunities to make mistakes and get feedback. Furthermore, because every student is an individual with a background, and experiences, and a future that will be unique to them, they need a classroom that is capable of responding to them.

Based on the research we know about learning, teachers who bring different strategies to help students find their own path to the correct answer, to find their way to a fruitful avenue to answer a question—is not only positive, it's really the only way we know successful learning happens.[19]

Now when you get asked why you teach innovatively with multiple methods of teaching and assessing beyond the usual lecture, papers, and exams—you can say (and write in your review materials) that it's because the biological basis for learning tells us that's the way to go!

The Case for Teaching and Assessing in Multiple Ways: It Creates the Student Engagement That Increases Learning

Finally, before moving on in the next section where I share words, phrases, and dialogue you can use when discussing your multiple teaching and assessment methods, let's hear from one more

SoTL expert about why teaching in an innovative way is the way to keep going.

An author of *Reach Everyone, Teach Everyone: Universal Design for Learning in Higher Education*,[20] Dr. Thomas J. Tobin, shares the following about what the science says about the student engagement that increases learning:

> The neuroscience behind it is that when we learn anything, we have to activate three different chemical pathways in our brains. We have to have the affective centers like the amygdala, the hippocampus, the inner parts of the brain, those things have to get activated and give us a reason to pay attention in the first place. This is the "why" of learning.
>
> When we learn new information or we see new things, or we're going to take on a new task, we have to have a reason to stay, get engaged and stay engaged. So if a pipe breaks under your kitchen sink, you have a reason to learn how to fix the pipe because there's water coming out and you need to stop that from happening. The why of learning is almost never that direct and clear. And the challenge for us is that we know the neuroscience behind why students don't get engaged and stay engaged with learning tasks. So, you have to [create student engagement to] turn on those brain networks that say, "Oh, I have a reason to learn this."[21]

An evidence-based method to get students engaged is to use a variety of strategies for teaching and assessment—especially those that get students actively involved.[22] These practices improve student learning because they engage students, which is part of the science of learning. And that's a good thing.

Now you know your authentic and strategic multipronged teaching and assessing approaches generate more knowledge transfer, and are built on the fundamentals of learning biology and the science of engagement and learning. But there's even more nourishment and empowerment for your teaching and academic career here.

The Case for Teaching and Assessing in Multiple Ways: Alignment with SoTL and Teaching Guidelines

In line with the above experts of SoTL, the SoTL teaching guidelines tell faculty to vary the practices we use to teach. A quick perusal turns up advice like this:

- "Use multiple teaching methods and modes of instruction."[23]
- Differentiated instruction "creates different learning paths so that students have the opportunity to learn as much as they can as deeply as they can."[24]
- "How do we get through most effectively to all students? Using a variety of methods allows the modality of instruction to be appropriately matched to the content being learned . . . [R]egardless of [the course topic] and how many class periods will be spent on it . . . try to present the topic in multiple ways to make it understandable to as many students as possible."[25]

This SoTL guidance very clearly states that teaching practices should be varied. And one reason to do so is that a static teaching method privileges students who learn best from that method. Which means that when you teach with multiple methods, you aren't just doing it for variety's sake. Using multiple and varied teaching methods allows more of the students in your courses to participate in the learning process.

Let's go deeper by taking a look at what the scholarship recommends for strategies to assess what students have learned:

- "There are many roads to learning. People bring different talents and preferences for learning to college. *Students need opportunities to show their talents* and learn in ways that work for them. Then they can be pushed to learn *[and demonstrate learning]* in *new ways* that do not come so easily." [emphasis added][26]
- "Vary your teaching strategies, *assignments and learning activities*. For example, give students opportunities to do group work as well as to work alone. *Provide options for assignments: written papers, oral reports and video* [. . .] Present the

same information in several modes (lecture, reading, audiovisual materials, and hands-on activities)." [emphasis added][27]
- "[M]ultiple measures can more accurately gauge student learning . . . multiple measures (a short essay, quiz, visual, and final project) allow you to better understand a student's level of progress . . . examine how you currently assess students. Are you using multiple measures, or do students have one shot to show you what they've learned? If you don't use multiple measures, how might you alter your course and its assessments to allow for a better, more holistic view of student learning on any given attribute? You'll end your course with a more complete understanding of student learning—and that's powerful and actionable data".[28]

Perhaps there are no real surprises here . . . the recommendation for assessing student learning is to adopt an assortment of strategies. Exactly what you're already doing! Your authentic ways of figuring out if and what students are learning makes you an innovative teacher in line with the SoTL. Not only does your use of multiple assessment strategies allow more students to demonstrate their learning but they also provide you with a fuller perspective on where students are. In doing this, you provide both support and challenge to students—both of which produce more student learning! All of that is going to look great in your teaching review materials. Boom!

What to Say to What They Say = Your Pushback to Their Pushback

It's time to celebrate your achievements—to allow your self-recognition to buoy you up. Because it's also time to draw a line on the pushback you've been getting for teaching the way you do. The research makes it plain that teaching innovation by women faculty of color has a myriad of positive consequences for student learning in a variety of areas, whether it's knowledge, skill, or cognitive development, moral development, or all of the above. Whatever learning outcome you can think of . . . students benefit when you mix it up versus relying upon only one teaching method or one way to assess.

This fact—grounded on a bedrock of data and decades of evidence—is your defense in conversations and reviews. Your pushback to anyone who pushes or pressures you to teach or assess their way. You let them know that your innovative use of a range of teaching methods produces increased and more robust student learning and assessment. And let them know with conviction, with the SoTL on the biology of learning, cognitive science, and universal learning design all having your back. Use all of these and the entirety of the SoTL as your defense if you experience any pushback, described in a prior section, that might sound like this:

- Colleagues: "We've always taught using lectures in this department. Maybe your negative teaching reviews and/or student ratings are because you don't lecture enough."
- Students: "I'm not doing well in this course because you don't teach. I don't pay to have discussions/group projects with other students. Why can't you just lecture like my other professors?!"
- Colleagues: "We've always given exams/research papers in this department. Maybe your negative teaching reviews and/or student ratings are because you assign case studies/field service/applied community projects/etc."
- Students: "I don't want to do a case study/field experience/group project/etc. because I don't do well with those things/it takes too much time/I don't pay tuition to waste my time on busywork. Can't I just write a paper/take an exam instead?!"
- Student ratings or colleague observation reports: "In [insert intro course that's been taught the same for decades], you include readings, activities, and/or assignments that are irrelevant/biased/your opinion/your political agenda."

When you get any sort of pushback, I encourage you to utilize the expertise, language, and guidance of the SoTL. This means creating scripts you should implement in reviews and conversations about your teaching—all to invoke scholarly research and literature as your shield. Here are a few concrete examples you should feel at liberty to use:

Example #1:

Yes, I understand that many in the department use lectures to teach, and you suggest I do the same, but MIT's teaching and learning center's guideline is to *"Use multiple teaching methods and modes of instruction."* Additionally, Miller's work on memory and learning supports this practice.[29] This is why I use additional methods to teach. Abiding by the SoTL instead of common conventions allows me to produce more student learning.

Example #2:

In their eponymous *Seven Principles for Good Practice in Undergraduate Education,* Chickering and Gamson highlight that "There are many roads to learning. People bring different talents and preferences for learning to college. Students need opportunities to show their talents and learn in ways that work for them. Then they can be pushed to learn in new ways that do not come so easily."[30]

Eyler's work on the varied biological paths to learning reflects related ideas. My teaching and assessment strategies are aligned with the SoTL. While my strategies may be less common or familiar, they reflect teaching excellence.

Example #3:

In response to the question "How do we get through most effectively to all students?" The American Psychological Association says: "Using a variety of methods allows the modality of instruction to be appropriately matched to the content being learned." The variety of teaching methods I use

REMAIN AUTHENTIC (AND INNOVATIVE) 129

"present the topic in multiple ways to make it understandable to as many students as possible." My doing so makes my teaching much more effective for student learning.

Example #4:

The longstanding authority on teaching, "Tools for Teaching" by Gross Davis, advises faculty to do the following: "Vary your teaching strategies, assignments and learning activities. For example, give students opportunities to do group work as well as to work alone. Provide options for assignments: written papers, oral reports and video [. . .] Present the same information in several modes (lecture, reading, audiovisual materials, and hands-on activities."[31]

Tobin and Behling's work on increasing student engagement to aid student learning makes similar points. So, while I know lecture and papers or exams are common, relying on those strategies runs contrary to the research and literature on the best teaching practices.

Example #5:

I assign more than papers or exams as "multiple measures can more accurately gauge student learning . . . multiple measures (a short essay, quiz, visual, and final project) allow you to better understand a student's level of progress." This way, students have more than one shot to demonstrate their learning in my courses. My assignments "allow for a better, more holistic view of student learning on any given attribute." Using this powerful teaching practice affords me "with a more complete understanding of student learning—and that's powerful and actionable data."

So you see! This sample language makes your teaching innovation even more evident for those chatting with you or reviewing your teaching for retention, tenure, or promotion. You mixing things up and veering away from the status quo is good for student learning and assessment. The guidance from the SoTL supports your innovative teaching. Keep using multiple strategies to teach and assess and push back on people who over rely on lectures and quizzes or exams.

SoTL Minefield:
A Caveat . . .

All of the above being said, I'd be remiss if I didn't mention a caveat. There is a gap—a glaring one that we want to be mindful of—in the SoTL. Yes, the research and guidance encourage you to be innovative by using multiple methods to teach and to assess. And it acknowledges that there will be some resistance and risk for doing so. But what it doesn't acknowledge is that women of color faculty, due to gendered racial oppression, won't have as much institutional power to protect themselves from that resistance and may not be as able to weather the risk of innovation to their academic careers.

The SoTL also does not assert the fact that institutions, for example department chairs, provosts, and teaching centers, must proactively support innovative women faculty of color (in addition to faculty in general). I call on SoTL scholars to research, advise, and advocate for institutional structures and policies that support vulnerable faculty who are more likely to be enacting that innovation. This is a significant way that institutions can proactively protect their women faculty of color from career sabotage. By doing so, the institution also proactively protects the authentic innovation and transformative teaching that is baked into the campus mission. So you must be aware of this gap. It isn't enough for the SoTL to advocate for teaching and assessment practices. Until their support happens and to fill the gap, you must confidently advocate for your innovative pedagogy choices both for your teaching and in your reviews.

Still . . . Keep Innovating

I hope you now know that you're not alone in your efforts to advance classroom success. The experts and guidance in the SoTL are clear that your use of multiple methods to teach and assess supports and increases learning. Your job now is to use all of the above evidence and research to own your excellence in your classroom and in reviews. Inoculate and protect yourself and your career with the data available. At the same time, be aware of the gaps where they exist in institutional policies and structures. A step at a time, we will generate the way forward to protect and support teaching innovation *and* vulnerable faculty such as Professor Michelle Jones who are more likely to be enacting that innovation. There is no reason why you or Professor Jones should experience less reward for innovative teaching than Professor White. Until that statement is true, I encourage you to tailor, edit, and practice the above illustrative talking points into your own voice and mold them to suit your teaching methods and vibe. Then use them in colleague conversations and teaching review materials! Doing so will help you get comfortable using the research and literature to repel the pressure to alter your teaching and protect your academic career.

Remember, this isn't just about silencing haters or those who don't understand the evidence-backed guidance for teaching practices. This is most importantly about fending off the negative consequences of their resistance, standing up for your teaching in reviews for the career you've worked so hard for, and to embody your pride and joy in your teaching. This is about you thriving with a successful academic career with less—or no—pushback.

Now keep on innovating! You're ready to continue your authentic teaching. You may still get pushback from students and colleagues but guess what? You don't have to just take it while others get rewarded for innovation. You can now pushback too using the research on women faculty of color's excellent teaching and the SoTL experts and guidance. Take full advantage of all of these things to bolster you to keep on teaching and assessing as you do, and more importantly to support your excellent teaching in renewal, tenure, and promotion reviews.

Summary

You should be proud—this chapter unequivocally designates your teaching and assessment strategies as innovative. When you need a reminder that your authentic teaching is the embodiment of the SoTL theory, revisit the following:

- Name your authentic teaching—your multiple strategies to teach and assess—for what it is: Teaching Innovation.
- Student and colleagues resist your and WFOC's innovative teaching more than they do to white and/or male faculty—who might indeed be rewarded (e.g., with tenure) for the same teaching you're punished for (e.g., denied tenure).
- Undeniable evidence-backed SoTL repels student and colleague resistance to your varied teaching and assessment strategies: (1) cognitive science of memory and learning, (2) biology of learning, (3) science of student engagement and learning, and (4) SoTL guidance.
- SoTL misses the mark by not recognizing, acknowledging, or broadcasting the additional challenges WFOC face for their teaching innovation.
- Proclaim your teaching innovation—that is to say, the use of multiple strategies—in your retention, tenure, and/or promotion materials.
- Your innovative teaching is the walk of the SoTL's talk.

Empowering Actions You Can Take This Week

This book will have maximum impact when you take action—what step might you take this week? The more you step in, the more you'll internalize and publicize that your amazing teaching should be celebrated and rewarded with retention/tenure/promotion!

Let's get that message out there! Share your most eye-opening moment from this chapter with #empoweredWFOC on the social media platform of your preference so more women faculty of color can feel empowered too!

1. How does it land with you that teaching innovation is simply anything different from lecture and papers or exams (i.e., the norm)?
2. Were you surprised to learn you are an innovative teacher? Make a list of the teaching and assessment strategies from this chapter that you already use. Now pat yourself on the back!
3. Take a look at the illustrative scripts in this chapter. Which might be useful to offset colleague or student resistance to your teaching innovation? Edit one to your voice and specific teaching innovations.
4. If you still think you aren't an innovative teacher or would like to discuss your experiences of resistance to your teaching and assessment methods or want my help identifying what's innovative about your teaching, especially to support your review—let's chat! Reach out to me at empowered@effectivefaculty.org.

Take full advantage of all of these things to bolster you to keep on teaching and assessing as you do, and more importantly to support your excellent innovative teaching in renewal, tenure, and promotion reviews. In the next chapter, we'll talk about why you must engage in joy to shift your energy away from draining racist and sexist teaching challenges and towards nourishing and replenishing engagement with yourself and what you love. Don't delay—get over to that chapter as soon as possible.

Chapter 6

CREATE JOY DESPITE EVERYTHING

Find out why you must infuse joy into your teaching experiences.

Uncover the teaching myths that drain the time and energy of women faculty of color.

Exhale with relief as you dismantle those myths, safeguard your career, and
redistribute reclaimed energy to anything and anyone you love.

△ *Here we are close to the end of the book and I have one last chapter for you that's at the heart of all we've covered so far. To get started, I'm going to ask you to try a visualization exercise. I'll guide you through step-by-step so just take a breath and read on.*

Take a slow, calming breath, and when you're ready, imagine yourself thriving in higher education.

What does that look like? Feel like? What do you see yourself doing?

... Can you see yourself laughing with students, enjoying their insights, and looking forward to your next conversation with them about the course material?

... What if chats with colleagues about your teaching innovations made you feel acknowledged, secure, and encouraged?

... Picture yourself skimming your course evaluations and teaching observation reports then tossing them aside to go about the rest of your day with a spring in your step.

... Now envision yourself proudly rewarded for your stellar teaching with retention, tenure, and promotion.

I hope you savor this visual for as long as you'd like, knowing there are many other women faculty of color reading this book imagining the same things. And feel free to return to this exercise at any time. It's part of your empowered teaching toolbox. △

Here's the thing. You absolutely can have this future in academe. It isn't a fantasy. Revel for a moment here in the idea of living in this glorious manner when it comes to your teaching experiences and academic career. It is possible! Women faculty of color can thrive despite the teaching challenges described in this book to earn retention/tenure/promotion. Now, you're probably wondering ... how do I get there? Thankfully, there are just two simple yet substantive steps:

1. Threats: Take a hard and close look at your current realities.

2. Strategic Actions: Make a commitment to do something different by enacting enacting the suggestions in this chapter.

Sounds easy enough, right? While this may sound too easy to be true, it is the truth about how you get closer to the teaching experiences that you desire. That said, I suspect some women of color might find these steps difficult. And others might respond with, "Say less. Done." There is plenty of room for the full range of reactions, so where does your reaction fall?

What's most important is that the steps sink in . . . just enough for you to take action on them. The steps are here for you to invest in doing so that you reach the campus experience and career success of your dreams that you wholeheartedly deserve. Ready? Take a deep breath and let's dive in.

Threat:
The Current Reality of the Beast

We're going to get to the good stuff soon. Before doing so we have to look the current reality of your teaching experience squarely in the eyes. I call it the Beast. The goal isn't to bum you out, rather to make it plain why joy and the strategies that produce it are not luxuries or extras but truly necessary.

Throughout the book we've talked about common teaching experiences for women faculty of color. In particular, we've examined how patterns of race and gender oppression show up as discriminatory and hostile challenges to women faculty of color's teaching and their reviews. Our teaching experiences are marred because we're more likely to be impacted by inappropriate student, colleague, and public challenges to our teaching scholarship, legitimacy, authority, and academic careers.

The statement that there are "structural challenges to women faculty of color's teaching" often looks sterile and objective. This language often strips away the tangible realities of oppression, keeping its ickiness at arm's length for those not personally affected by it. As a reminder, here's what this ickiness looks like in the words of actual women faculty of color:

> "White, cisgendered, heterosexual male students critique my accent, my looks, and my body."
>
> "Colleagues often criticize my teaching as being racist or focusing on race too much. It got so bad I had to add an entire section in my tenure application to heavily emphasize that all of my teaching is based on research."
>
> "A student reporter sent one of my course readings to a tv/radio host and this resulted in misleading and antagonistic coverage of me and my teaching on both platforms."
>
> "Students have not spoken in class as a silent protest. They repeatedly call me Mrs. even though I repeatedly ask them to call me Dr. They interrogate my basic qualifications and competence, going so far as to say 'this professor knows nothing' on my evals."
>
> "Colleagues and students have said that my class was just a part of the _____ agenda. So they don't approve of the assignments or grades calling them 'biased' or 'non-objective.' And this sort of opposition tends to increase when the topics of discussion include minoritized identities of any kind."
>
> "I've had two incidents of verbal aggression from students and one fearful incident of a student threatening me."
>
> "I was hit in the face by an angry 'liberal' colleague who was upset about my inclusive teaching practices."

As you read this chapter, keep the above real-life examples in the forefront of your mind rather than any bloodless academic labels like "structural challenges to women faculty of color." It's vitally important that you don't let the technical terms sanitize the lived experiences of the teaching challenges you and your career face. The "cleaned up" language conspires to distance you from acting to offset the reality you're up against. And we simply can't have that, m'kay?

Energy Required to Tussle with the Beast

In order to understand the fullness of the need for joy, we need to acknowledge that managing raced and gendered dynamics requires additional labor. That is, on top of the labor all faculty must expend to teach—you must expend additional labor to navigate, strategize, and survive the structural mess of race and gender in your classroom.

Let's talk a bit about labor and load. Most people think of labor primarily as time—the time you spend doing this task or that task. The butt in the seat time of preparing for teaching, grading, and meeting with students. Yes, time is one way to describe the additional labor and overload of women faculty of color.

But that isn't the only labor and load we are overburdened with. To ensure that you understand and can talk about the energy and labor required by your teaching, let's talk about three specific forms of invisible labor and load: Cognitive, Affective, and Emotional labor. Understanding these will help you to more quickly pursue and achieve the joyful experiences I want you to have.

COGNITIVE LABOR

Simply put, cognitive labor is the thinking, planning, strategizing, and problem-solving you do to keep your teaching up and running. As women faculty of color, we have to expend additional cognitive labor to address the challenges of race and gender oppression in our classrooms and reviews. For example, as represented in this Asian-American women faculty's own words:

> "I feel the need to over perform in the classroom. And this wouldn't be the case if I wasn't one of the few minority faculty members at my teaching focused institution."

She describes the additional cognitive labor she and other women faculty of color engage in to "overperform" in their classrooms. It takes cognitive labor (i.e., thinking, anticipating, strategizing, problem-solving) to teach at the performance level that is above the abysmal expectations that students and colleagues have of women faculty of color. And this faculty member is acutely aware that this added cognitive labor is necessary only because she is a woman of color. Sound familiar? Do you overperform? Can you start to see that only by acknowledging this can we properly employ the tools for creating joy and renewal?

Or maybe this real-life illustration sounds more familiar:

"Teaching is something fun and enjoyable for me, but having to deal with so many unjustifiable challenges is exhausting, and it takes all the fun and joy out of teaching."

This Black woman faculty member thoroughly enjoys teaching but is drained by the disproportionate challenges and sapped of her joy. She is typical of a lot of my clients. Do you enjoy teaching but feel similarly exhausted? No cognitive labor left for research, grants, or loved ones because you're exhausted? Below is one more illustration in a woman of color faculty's own words of the cognitive labor women of color are expending that their dominant status peers are not:

"I have struggled to make the best sustainable choices. Like how hard should I work to make sure my evals are good in the face of resistant/racist students? This semester I had great evals, but I worked like crazy with respect to teaching."

Whew! I bet this one hit a nerve! A lot of my clients engage in non-stop thinking and strategizing about the biased student evaluations they receive. Rightfully so since these problematic evaluation scores and comments are often seized upon to deny their retention, tenure, and/or promotion bids. In plain language, these discriminatory eval scores and comments can destroy the academic careers of women faculty of color. So it should come as no surprise that they might spend the entire 12 to 16 weeks of the academic term anticipating, strategizing, and problem-solving in their teaching to counter the racism and sexism in their evals. No wonder we are worn out!

While all cognitive labor won't exactly look like these women of color's actual words and lived experiences above, I'm sure you should get the point:

> [. . .] cognitive labor entails anticipating needs, identifying options for filling them, making decisions, and monitoring progress [. . .] such work is taxing but often invisible to both cognitive laborers and [others].[1]

Any labor that you spend to anticipate, strategize, and problem-solve for the unique teaching challenges described in this book is cognitive labor. It is often invisible, very taxing, and labor that others do not have to spend.

Let's keep this recognizing and naming train going by talking about another form of invisible labor you are likely unfairly saddled with in your classroom and reviews. Once we have this under our belts, we're going to get to your happier classroom and review experiences.

AFFECTIVE LABOR

Affective labor is the work you do to manage students' emotions in your classroom and about your teaching. An outsider might wonder "What do emotions have to do with teaching? Just teach the content!". Yet many women faculty of color are aware that managing students' emotions—for example, fear, anxiety, anger/frustration, sadness, excitement, boredom, confusion—is an integral part of teaching (and learning). This labor should be expected of all faculty but gender expectations mean that students, administrators, and colleagues most frequently demand additional amounts of affective work from women faculty.[2] And when we add race and racism in the classroom to the maddening expectation pie, this results in even more affective labor put onto the shoulders of women of color especially relative to peers with dominant statuses.[3] I hear you saying, "You mean white male faculty don't spend lots of labor on students' emotions in the classroom, say what?" That's right, that is what I'm saying. Here's an illustration shared by a Filipina instructor:

"The biggest issues have been getting them over their discomfort with the material on diverse others and getting them to see the world differently."

This Filipina instructor may not realize it but she is perfectly pinpointing affective labor. She is describing the affective labor she has to expend to move students past their emotional discomfort with course material that includes diverse and multiple perspectives. A faculty member who has dominant social statuses and/or doesn't teach diverse perspectives in their course content doesn't have to expend this additional labor. Ugh. How about another illustration from the lived experience and words of a woman of color faculty member?

"I received noticeably more hostility from students around race, gender, sexual orientation when teaching."

Instead of students accepting the discomfort that results from legitimate learning, this Black woman is having to use additional affective labor to manage their emotions and outright hostility. White male faculty may require labor to manage student frustration, confusion, or fear as expected components of student learning. But the odds are less that they are forced to labor to quell outright hostility from students.

Unfortunately it is more common for women faculty of color to face hostility in their teaching such as student outbursts, verbal attacks, or physical aggression.[4] Which means that we have to put out extraneous effort to manage and influence student's hostile affect. And this additional affective labor siphons away from the labor we need for other scholarly products (e.g., publications).

Just one final real-world illustration. Let's talk about a different type of student emotion that demands affective labor from women faculty of color:

> "I told a white female student that some of her comments about African countries were culturally insensitive. Many tears in that meeting. She ran out and the issue was never resolved."

The tears! That's right, white tears are another example of when affective labor is required more often of women faculty of color. Again, while male faculty are less expected to "care" for crying students, gender expectations mean this is readily expected of women faculty.[5] And at the interplay of race and gender expectations—whoo wee—women of color are expected to labor to place whites' emotions above their own, dropping everything to care for them even when they've engaged in harmful behaviors.[6]

This is the affective labor that needs to be alleviated in order to create the teaching vibe and successful reviews of your dreams! Just one more type of labor overload in the way of those dreams.

EMOTIONAL LABOR

The final type of labor you apply in your teaching is emotional labor. This is the effort you use to produce, modify, or repress your own emotions while teaching. Of course every instructor likely has a moment or two when they fake, project, or stuff down an emotion. However, women faculty of color have to shell out more of this emotional labor and more frequently than their peers due to the high-pressure scenarios colleagues and students put them in.[7] Let's take a look at a few examples in women of color's own words:

> "I have one white male student who challenges my authority non-stop. My chair told me he is an admirer of Hitler [and genocide] so I am careful and scared of him."

This Black woman professor experiences constant and inappropriate disruptions from this student. Yet she cannot express her emotions of rightful indignation, frustration, or whatever emotion she feels about it. Instead of offering her classroom protection from these disruptions to learning, her chair warned her of the student's admiration of genocide. Say what now?! So she is forced to engage in emotional labor to teach while hiding her indignation, fear, and apprehension. I am exhausted and nervous just thinking about her having to engage this student day in and day out in her classroom. Can you imagine how much labor she has to waste "presenting" emotionally in a way that keeps her safe? Whew! Exhale with me and let's look at another teaching scenario:

> *"I am extremely uncomfortable with some of the male students' extreme interest in me and my body, as well as their frequent emails."*

Unlike this Latina, privileged faculty rarely experience harassment from students (e.g., contrapower harassment). Accordingly, privileged colleagues, campus norms, and institutional policies often don't recognize, validate, or accept that contrapower harassment even occurs. In light of this, to not be seen (again) as a deficient teacher who somehow brought the harassment upon herself, this Latina engages in emotional labor to teach and engage these male students as though nothing is problematic, out of place, or unusual.

Can you think of experiences in which you endure troublesome student interactions by recasting your emotional reactions as part of your usual routine? Or to offset potential teaching threats to your teaching evaluations, observations, or reviews?

You may find it interesting that circumstances that require your emotional labor aren't alway overtly negative or extreme. Here is a common scenario we face as described by another woman of color faculty member:

> *"I'm overwhelmed with teaching/mentoring students of color and the university doesn't value my emotional labor devoted to supporting these students. Instead, they emphasize pandering to and keeping students happy in courses with large enrollments despite how hostile these students are in the classroom."*

I am not sure what's most jarring in this all-too-common illustration of how women of color have to modify their emotions. That they have to trudge through their overwhelm and exhaustion—without university support or relief—to support marginalized students. Or that the university pushes them to fake whatever emotions are necessary to keep students happy. Both are quite problematic. The university boasts its support for marginalized students, yet rarely assists or compensates the women of color who provide it.[8] Even if we enjoy this work or view it as our duty, the expenditure of emotional labor for students of color is not sustainable, with many of us putting on a brave face despite overwhelm and burnout. And this overwhelm introduces risks to both our well-being and the productivity required for reviews. Our institutions are creating even more of a demand for your emotional labor by compelling women of color to be "nice," "nurturing," and pander to student demands. And all of this is expected despite bad student behavior that should allow women of color to express a fuller and more authentic range of emotional responses.

Consequences of Tussling with the Beast (i.e., Expending So Much Extra Labor)

Let's take a deep breath together and return to why I've shared all of this in the first place. I'm not doing so to needlessly be a Debbie Downer. My goal as always is to empower you to stand strongly in your teaching excellence and reviews. To do so in this instance, I'm making sure you are intimately familiar with the types of labor demanded by your teaching first so we can thoroughly address how joy must play a role in offsetting this for you. Familiarity with the additional labor and painful consequences for your work helps to move you towards a thoroughly healthier teaching and academic career future!

Faculty with privileged statuses are required to impart cognitive, affective, and emotional labor in their teaching too. But, you are required to do so disproportionately and continuously such that it becomes the status quo. For this reason, we as women faculty of color often don't recognize these expectations as burdening work, labor, or energy.

Of course, the toll of all this cognitive, affective, and emotional labor from you has negative physical and mental health outcomes as well:[9]

- Disordered sleep
- Depression
- High blood pressure
- Cardiovascular disease
- Anxiety
- Job satisfaction
- Job commitment

Not surprisingly, the stress of this inordinate amount of labor the institution places on you also has negative outcomes for the students you teach:[10]

- Increased student stress (e.g., increased cortisol) when instructor stress increases
- Lowered academic performance
- Lowered engagement
- Reduced motivation
- Reduced achievement
- Increased disruptive behavior
- Lowered sense of belonging
- Lessened belief in ability to succeed
- Lower grades

All in all, you are expending additional labor navigating the challenges in this book on top of the extra labor you use to teach, mentor, and advise students. The consequences of all of this work leaves you with minimal time and ability to be present for yourself, serve others, enjoy your family and friends. It also means that your career duties (e.g., grants, publications, research)—no matter how dedicated you are—are negatively impacted because the well of labor, work, and energy is dry.

SoTL Minefield:
Perpetuation of Labor Inequalities for Women Faculty of Color

When it comes to creating the optimal teaching environment, and an empowered academic career for us, it's regrettable but true, the SoTL often makes the inequitable teaching situation for women faculty of color worse. It does so by perpetuating the myth of teachers as martyrs; by normalizing that everything is and should be student-centered; by writing about teachers as though we don't have needs of our own. That teachers should tie themselves to the railroad tracks—and the train is students and teaching—and that yes, it runs you over and you should be happy about it. I'm pushing back against that and I hope legions of you will join me.

On top of martyrdom being normalized—privileged groups have the ability to opt out of lots of labor without penalty. For example, men aren't expected to perform the "care" that many interpret as "mothering" and yet are not seen as an inferior teacher for doing so. The cognitive, emotional, and affective labor required for teachers to "care" as per the SoTL is an expectation that most frequently falls on the shoulders of women faculty.[11] Mix that gendered expectation with race and you end up with women of color who are expected to be caretakers for students.

All of this means all of those labor-intensive "caring" and "compassion" norms in the SoTL are applied to us even more so than they're applied to white faculty. The narrative language about that intensive labor may appear a bit hidden in words like "caring" and "available" and "approachable," "responsive," "trauma-informed," "student-centered," "nurturing," , etc.—which are essentially code words for the labor women and especially women of color faculty are expected to shoulder more than anyone else.[12]

It would be helpful to women of color if the SoTL made it plain that:

1. educational and pedagogical "caring" for students doesn't mean "mothering" and

2. colleagues and students should stop making inappropriate gendered and raced demands on our labor.

Essentially, instead of leaving us out here unprotected, we need SoTL scholars to tell colleagues and administrators to not expect, side-eye, nor punish women faculty of color when they do less of this labor, in alignment with the lesser amount of this labor delivered by faculty with privileged status such as white males.

Getting to the Teaching Future You Deserve and Want

At the start of this chapter, I asked you to envision yourself thriving in higher education. Specifically, I again want you to imagine yourself having a ton of wonderful teaching experiences like:

- laughing with students about the course material
- affirming conversations with colleagues about your innovative teaching
- surrounding yourself with a healthy and joyful bubble in the classroom that minor injustices don't penetrate, and
- a successful career where you've received retention, tenure, or promotion.

Yes—you can have all of this and more! I know—we just went over the massive expenditure of labor you spend to deal with racism and sexism in your teaching experiences. We did so, not as evidence that future positive teaching experiences are impossible, but as evidence that your future MUST be different. That added labor is unsustainable. And hopefully that examination has persuaded you to be on a mission to create joy and career protection in the face of that. I want to check in with you for a moment:

- How are you at this moment, really?
- Do you have even a small amount of bandwidth to consider how you can access joy and protection a little each day going forward?

- Can I entice you to commit to doing something different—however small to start—in order to generate different outcomes?
- Maybe you have the experience of not being sure what needs to change.

By now I hope you know I've got you covered! Let's now turn to several strategies that will improve your teaching experiences and move you far, far away from exhausting fatalistic labor so you can use that labor however you so choose (research productivity, rest, joy, etc.). Can I get a heck yes?!

Tame the Labor Beast and Make Space for a Different Teaching Future

The overall strategy is one you may feel is incredibly counterintuitive. But I want you to listen closely because it really is important:

You must reduce the time, energy, and labor you spend on teaching.

Okay, I'll pause. I know, that's a bold statement and might be hard to take in. Let's stay with it. To be clear, no, I'm not suggesting you become a bad teacher, lower your teaching quality, or neglect students. Not even one bit. In fact, what I'm suggesting is supporting you to spend less time teaching and maintain (or even improve) standards, while reducing lack of productivity risks to your career. It can be done, but it will require adjustments on your part.

In the face of the many teaching inequities you encounter, using less energy on teaching must sound both impossible and unwise. Shouldn't you spend time and energy to remain vigilant and fend off adversaries? Shouldn't you work hard to make all aspects of your teaching—course material, lectures, learning activities, grading, etc.—bulletproof? The issue is that this boundless use of time and energy is not sustainable nor successful. No amount of time that you as an individual pour into teaching will eliminate the systemic oppression you face. You can't fix a problem like tomato blight by painstakingly washing one tomato, right? This knowledge should shift your goal from eliminating what you cannot control (i.e., racism and sexism) to the goal of teaching with as efficient use of labor as possible. This helps you go from pouring into a limitless, bottomless, and thankless bucket to, let's say, filling a regular-sized cereal bowl. And doing this will leave time and energy for your joy (and other career demands). This is a goal that you CAN impact and control. Now we are onto something!

There are plentiful SoTL "how to" items and I offer courses and coaching on how to spend less time on teaching. Yet, these are not useful if you're not yet convinced or you have nervousness about dialing back your teaching time and labor. It is absolutely possible and actually evidence-based to allot less time on teaching, produce resultant excellent teaching . . . and then get the heck out of that space mentally and physically. Do a great job and remove yourself from toxicity as fast as possible! This is one of my favorite things to support you with. All I want to hear is you saying "Heck yea! I'm gonna take advantage of resources to reduce my teaching labor." I'm going to assume you're saying that, and I hope that's true.

With that opening in place for you, let's take on a couple of myths that might be blocking you—but hopefully not for long.

Threat:
Myths about Teaching Time and Energy

Myth: Great teaching requires tons of time and energy.

Truth: Efficient teaching is Great teaching.

Surprised at this truth? You're not alone. But the scholarship is clear. Spending an oversized amount of time and energy on teaching (aka overpreparing) is linked to several negative outcomes for students.[13] Overprepping results in more course content than students can consume,[14] so all of that "extra" content you dedicated so much time to preparing goes to waste and creates student frustration and angst. Also, while you anxiously throw everything and the kitchen sink at them, students are impacted by your panicked energy. Trying to squeeze all that content into what seems like not enough teaching time doesn't lead to good things.

The same ideas apply to grading! The precious time you overinvested to provide lots of feedback? The more you throw at students the less they're able to make sense of it;[15] and when you're stressed about grading, you add to students' stress about grading.[16] The larger lesson to learn here is that teaching labor reaches a point of diminishing returns. The more time and energy you put into it, the less and less you get in return. And once you get past a certain point, you'll start to see negative returns.

Guess what women faculty of color do NOT need in their classroom? More emotionally activated students who are anxious, frustrated, angstful, confused, or stressed. This is a recipe for classroom incivility akin to adding kerosene to the already combustible dynamics of race and gender oppression in the classroom.

You can pour as much time and energy as you like into your teaching, but don't fool yourself that you'll see a similar return in student outcomes (e.g., learning). Excessive time on teaching isn't how you "fix" or address gendered racist teaching inequities.[17]

So, NO, tons of time and energy spent on teaching isn't the marker of great teaching. It's the marker of misspent, misused, and squandered time and energy. Instead, let's encourage you to embrace the opposite—the support you need to create an intentionally efficient use of time and energy to produce great teaching and better student outcomes.[18] In short, efficient teaching produces a reasonable amount of course content for students to learn and calm teaching with students who mirror that energy back. This is a formula for fewer classroom incivilities for you, greater student learning, and more time and energy for you to allocate as you need or choose.

Are you in the business of throwing away your time and energy and harming student outcomes? No? Then stop using exorbitant time and energy on teaching starting today and you will be on your way to creating more joy and academic success. Done and done.

Myth: Spending a lot of time and energy on teaching is how you show care for students.

Truth: Pedagogical care for students doesn't require a huge investment of time and energy.

The messaging we get about teaching is that the only way to show care, compassion, and dedication to students is to selflessly dedicate our time and energy to it. This messaging makes faculty feel like they are abandoning or neglecting students when they aren't spending an exorbitant amount of time on teaching. And it also causes our peers to shame us when we limit our time on teaching. But guess what, we don't have time to pay attention to them. Do you see all the affective, emotional, and cognitive labor women of color are pressured to spend on teaching?[19] Don't let students, administrators, or colleagues trip you up or continue to put the weight of care, mentoring, or advising students on your shoulders. You MUST reduce your teaching labor or you will burn out and risk not being retained, tenured, or promoted. You won't make it in higher education and that is definitively not what we're after.

I will attempt to make this even clearer by sharing the truth. Newsflash: There is nothing in the SoTL that says care for students is equated to dedicating a mountain of time and energy towards teaching. In fact, quite the opposite is true. Whether you're aiming for care, connection, presence, sense of belonging, immediacy, etc. in your teaching—the SoTL frequently provides discrete practices that are easy and fast to implement.[20] For example, it commonly suggests:

- address students by name (e.g., start with table placards or videoconference name displays)
- communicate clear expectations and explicit instructions (e.g., syllabus, due date reminders), and
- get to know students as unique individuals (e.g., ask students questions about themselves), etc.

That's it. Simple, right? No requirements for excessive time in order to demonstrate the care that aids student learning. The key ingredient for this relational dynamic is that your course planning, learning goals, and teaching practices are *intentional*. With a clear understanding and anticipation of students' learning needs, you can put practices in place in much less time. These will improve outcomes much more so than any pandering, coddling, or mothering that some mistake for pedagogical care.

In other words, it is absolutely your choice to coddle, cater to, and mother students. Just don't mistake or equate that chosen labor for the pedagogical care you are required to provide in your professional role as an instructor. They are not interchangeable nor the same. And it won't substitute for the tangible products you'll need for a successful review.

Now let's get deeper into the good stuff that'll lead you to your teaching and career aspirations! It's essential that, as women faculty of color, we teach efficiently and nourish ourselves with a full range of professional and personal goals. Here's a straightforward and quick way to get you started on your efficient (and effective) teaching journey.

Strategic Action:
Start to Reduce Your Teaching Time and Energy

Examine your course topics. When I coach faculty on streamlining their courses, many attempt to teach too much material. So you must leave behind the "everything but the kitchen sink" approach.

Instead use these brainstorm prompts to narrow and reduce your course topics (and thus teaching time):

- Key concepts?
- Theories/theorists?
- Classic or contemporary works?
- Necessary skill competencies?
- Controversies in the field?

> The results of this quick brainstorm are the essential and ONLY topics you should cover in your course. Mercilessly and ruthlessly cut everything that falls outside of what you've identified here as your core content.

Haven't identified anything you think you can cut? Here's my tough love for you. That's just your resistance, fear, and comfort zone speaking. Brainstorm again and list the indispensable answers to the prompts and ignore the "might be nice" ones. And yes, you can still focus and narrow your course content in this manner even with an externally established curriculum, licensure, and accreditation, requirements, and/or dependent course sequences.

Teaching too much material isn't a good thing or a badge of honor. In fact, it harms both students and faculty members. Students can only learn a reasonable amount of information.[21] Similarly, faculty can only prepare, teach, and assess a reasonable amount of information.[22] Using these two realities, you are not shortchanging students when you enhance their ability to learn the core and essential disciplinary material by reducing your course's content.

> **Nervous and need to scale back a little at a time?**
>
> If it'd make you feel better, you can leave the material cut via the brainstorm in the course as supplementary readings, an extra-credit assignment, options for a course unit whose topic is decided by students or as possible research/project/paper topics. You can even use the cut course topics to pitch or design a new "advanced" version of the original course.

Strategic Action:
Start to Reduce Your Outlay of Teaching Labor

It's time to measure! Because it's the best way to make substantive progress here. So track your student-care labor.

Track the (1) specific tasks and (2) time you spend on each of those tasks while "caring" for students for one week. Once the tracking is completed, take a look at the total amount of labor you expended on student care. Is it an amount of time that allows you to also care for yourself each week? Can you also conduct the amount of research you need for a successful retention or tenure review? How about working on grants required for your salary? The amount of time you spend on teaching must also accommodate the number of publications you must write to position yourself for promotion. Not to mention spend ample quality time with your family, friends, and loved ones for your mental and emotional well-being.

If you said "Yes, I have ample time and energy for these 'student care' items," feel free to ignore what follows here.

But if your answer is "No, I need more time/energy for my research and loved ones," then you must use your time tracking to identify the #1 specific "caring" task that comprised *most* of your labor during the week.

Now take a close hard look at that caring task that takes up the *most* of your time, energy, and labor. Is it an example of an evidence-based pedagogical caring strategies (immediacy, connection, presence, rapport, etc.)—*as defined by the research literature?* For example:[23]

- Eye contact
- Positive nonverbal communication (e.g., smile, gesture, nod)
- Casual sharing/banter/chats
- Clear, consistent communication
- Timely and actionable feedback on assignments
- Include a few (to your comfort level) personal details in your introduction
- Communicate care about their well-being
- Chat with students briefly before and after class
- Express interest in students' lives
- Gather information about student and their interests
- Students' interests included in all aspects the course (e.g., material, objectives, assignments, facilitation)

While the pedagogical care, sense of belonging, connection, etc. behaviors above are simple and non-time intensive, they are backed up by the research as effective.

If your major caring task consumes a lot of your energy yet is not listed among the pedagogical care items above ... but something else ... it's simple. It's time to adjust, delete, and reduce. Not because you don't care about students but because you care about yourself, your career, AND the students. The truth is that the caring tasks that take up the most of your effort are often misaligned with the scholarship and teaching literature AND may not even be producing the support and success outcomes you desire.

> **Begin to reduce your teaching labor by acting upon the answers to this question ... how can you cut, redirect, or delegate the "caring" labor task that eats away *most* of your time and energy?**
>
> Seriously, in your gut and heart of hearts, what do you know you can cut or delegate, even if you have inner resistance but know you would benefit from? Start there.

Remember while this labor might feel good to you (and students), the literature demonstrates they aren't central to (diverse) student support or success. Is that good feeling (without its intended student outcomes) worth you losing your career? Health? Family? Joy?

Reclaim Your Time, Energy, and Labor

Now you have a place to start these time, energy, and labor reductions! The sooner you start to engage in the above actions, the better! You'll have created more space and time away from teaching toxicity, reduced your and students' angst, and freed up time to engage in career supporting, life giving, sustenance, and restorative activities both in and outside of the classroom! I hope you get it—and I hope you understand my enthusiasm.

In just a moment, we'll move along to talk about restorative teaching actions you can put in the space, time, and energy you just freed up by making your teaching more efficient!

Enacting the above strategic actions to reduce your teaching time and labor leads to *higher* student engagement, *enhanced* classroom climate, *improvements* in student perception of instructor care, presence, and connection, and *increases* in student learning. And thankfully so because guess what can also result from this labor reduction? Less time on teaching = less time in a toxic space = lessened negative influence of your confrontative teaching experiences on you and your career. Dial it back, reduce your labor, and create the teaching and career reality of your dreams!

Nourishing and Sustaining YOU While Teaching

Now I want to share another strategy you can use in the face of inequitable labor loads. It's this:

You must increase the time, energy, and labor you spend to nourish, replenish, restore, and sustain YOU.

It's understandable that raced and gendered teaching obstacles weigh you down with anger, worry, stress, preoccupation, etc. This labor is undeniable and you must acknowledge it. But this isn't where your story ends. None of this extra cognitive, affective, or emotional load is good for your mind, spirit, or body. Which means that you wallow OR ignore it to your detriment.

Instead, you must be intentional about restoring what you lose as a result of this labor. You must nourish yourself at all times so your well is full when the bumps hit. Strategic action is important, not only to reduce the inequitable labor you expend, but to allow you to reclaim time and energy to engage in what sustains you in the face of drains. To get and stay empowered, you must engage in joy, especially in your teaching.

Feeling resistant to the idea that you need to do this? Think that you'll be just fine without this strategy? Let's dispel that resistance by tackling the myth that might be keeping you stuck on empty, burnt out, and overwhelmed.

Threat:
Myth about Faculty Needs

Myth: Students' wants and needs are the most important, above all else.

Truth: Faculty and students both have needs—both are important facets of student learning.

Are you thinking: "Of course students come first!" or "Whoa, isn't it taboo to say this truth aloud?" Ha! Whether you believe this indoctrinated untruth or fear backlash for calling this myth out as false, you can't deny that higher education often communicates the expectation that students' wants and needs come FIRST above anything else. And in fact, higher education communicates that students' wants and needs are the ONLY ones that matter.

It should be glaringly obvious what's wrong with this sentiment. Uh, duh—student wants and needs aren't the only item in the equation that is higher education. By prioritizing these at all costs, we neglect a principal ingredient. Faculty needs. Just like the omnipresent recommendation when flying on a plane. If you don't put your own oxygen mask on first, you will be of no use to whoever you may be trying to assist. So it goes in the classroom if you don't put your own needs into the mix. Of course, this myth is especially harmful for women faculty of color whose teaching labor is already being consumed like a black hole by higher education,[24] often leaving us as hollowed, sucked dry, barely hanging on, harried, and jobless versions of ourselves.[25] We're already oxygen-deprived to begin with.

This myth produces neglect of, exhaustion in, and burnout for women faculty of color. These conditions aren't sustainable, they sacrifice our careers, and they serve no one. Ignoring faculty needs actually works against the student learning that higher education attempts to prioritize. To get the desired outcomes for students, higher education must attend to faculty wants and needs as an additional priority. Since the myth disproportionately affects the consumption of your labor and neglects your and women faculty's needs, this shift by higher education is especially important for your academic success and overall well-being. But institutional change is slow which means that YOU must attend to your wants and needs and do it NOW. If you don't do it—who will?

No one is coming to help put your oxygen mask on, except maybe each other—the community of women faculty of color that I hope will be galvanized by these ideas.

Strategic Action:

Start to Nourish/Restore/Rejuvenate Yourself in the Classroom

Excited to start inserting joy into your teaching?! What's one simple way to start? Identify what makes you feel successful or satisfied in the classroom. For example, what's something that students do or say that make you feel accomplished or happy? Or what is something you enjoy in your regular life outside of the classroom? How might you incorporate that into the classroom?

Whatever your answer is to any or all of these questions needs to be embedded on a regular basis into your teaching and classroom. These cannot occur as unicorns, happenstance, or randomly. If these moments feed you, you have the opportunity to proactively embed them into your teaching—intentionally and frequently. This starts to get exciting.

What might that look like?

> *Professor Brown was tickled with glee when—at the start of class—a student shared a skit from a short format video that was related to course content. She spent 5–10 minutes of class with students watching and discussing the clip. It energized the students for the rest of that class session and the one after it too! And multiple students wrote positively about it on her evaluations.*

In my conversations with Dr. Brown, it was apparent that she got a kick out of students making connections between the real world and the course material on their own. I encouraged her to plan this dynamic into the course material so that it was a predictable jolt of joy rather than a moment that occurred once in a blue moon. She adjusted the format of class so that the first ten minutes of class were regularly dedicated to students sharing and chatting about whatever they felt was connected to the course material. This wasn't a required assignment; rather students were incentivized (e.g., extra credit, participation points, flexible deadline token, etc.) to participate. They were also openly rewarded (e.g., verbal or written praise/compliments) when they shared an item to discuss. This slight change provided Dr. Brown with regular dopamine rushes in her student interactions instead of previously being drained by them.

If your teaching is so stressful you can't even recall a moment of success or joy from it, you aren't alone. Dr. Raquel Saddiq was in that situation, yet I was able to suggest a way she could insert a bit of elation into her teaching experiences:

Raquel beamed with pride as her colleague asked about the excited chatter she'd overheard from students in her course. Yes! Students were so pumped that their interest and engagement had spilled outside of her classroom. And what Dr. Saddiq's colleague overheard made it into her reviews as evidence of teaching excellence.

Dr. Saddiq's secret? She added something SHE loved to her teaching. Gardening. In her humanities course, students were intrigued by Raquel noting women's relationships and positions to their gardens. Even if the students' curiosity hadn't been piqued, this insertion built a container within which Dr. Saddiq could revel and roll around in the pastime she loves!

It's easy to see that gardening is relevant to courses in STEM, humanities, social science, fine arts, health, education, etc. And it's a good illustration that whatever your joy, it's also likely relevant to your disciplinary perspective as well. The logistics of how you bring it into your teaching is up to you. Podcast episode, quote, image, song, discussion, lecture, etc. It just shouldn't be complicated, high stakes, or labor-intensive as this would suck the light out of it for you and students. The point isn't to build a new activity or course, so don't do that. The logistics of how to add YOUR peace or invigoration into the classroom are open to your joyful imagination!

Remember, our goal is for you to replace some of the stressful teaching labor you reduced with fulfilling, positive, and restorative teaching energy. And you do this by adding something you enjoy. Where is it written that this isn't allowed? This will fuel and sustain you for both your academic and personal well-being. The alternative to inserting joy is to continue to exist in a space that is hostile. You have everything to gain by heeding this likely novel suggestion. In fact, the research suggests that doing so increases instructor–student connection, student engagement, learning outcomes (e.g., synthesis and application), etc.[26]

Now it's your turn. What do you find restorative that might be incorporated into ten minutes of your next class for a bit of respite?

Find and Reclaim Your Joy

If nothing else in this chapter has landed, at least leave with this message:

You must engage in joy.

You may be thinking "I don't have time for that!" And I get it, right? What I've observed over the years is that it's especially hard for women of color to think about joy in the midst of all the "things" that we have to face. We feel guilty because there is so much work to be done and so much struggle to be addressed. We feel like it's a luxury for us to engage in joy when other people are struggling or our loved ones need us. A lot of times it feels like joy isn't allowed nor is it within our reach.

What I'm telling you is that . . . joy is allowed. It is required. It is essential. We're not going to survive without engaging in some type of joy. So, engage in joy inside and outside your classroom.

I understand if you still don't quite hear what I'm saying but I hope you'll try anyway. Historically, we haven't been given the space to engage in joy. No one has allowed it, no one has encouraged it and in some cases it has even been prohibited. Instead, we get the message that we have to sacrifice ourselves for others. That our worth is defined by what we're doing for others versus what we must do to maintain ourselves. Which is why I'm here telling you the opposite.

If you believe your purpose on this earth is to serve others—how can you do so if you're not here to do it? No energy? No mental space? Physically ill? Job loss so no finances? You can't be there for the people and causes you love when you're not well or when you yourself are depleted. Pause and think for a second. How have you been showing up for the things you say you're serving? Are you really serving them? Are you exhausted, are you irritable, are you giving them the best that you have to give? I suspect the answer to that is no.

Here are two of my favorite expressions: "You can't water others while you're withering on the vine" and "You can't pour from an empty cup." Both communicate that it isn't sustainable to constantly serve others without balance or restoration.

Rather than being pushed out of the university, pushed out of good health, merely surviving, exhausted and dragging yourself into campus and home—how about you instead make space (i.e., reduce teaching labor) and engage in joy (i.e., add restorative teaching moments)?

Instead of your current reality let's get you to a future where your teaching includes whatever you define as success and intentional moments of peace. This is the future I wish for you. Where you are a thriving, whole, successful, and healthy academic and human being.

Summary

In this chapter, I took you from your teaching fantasies to ick realities then back to those fantasies that can become your new realities. I am excited for you to take the strategic actions in it so you can transform those teaching fantasies into your actuality!

Keep these key points in mind as you journey towards joy inside and outside of teaching:

- You can have the joyful, healthier, and happier teaching and successful career of your dreams—yes, despite and in the face of colleagues and students who are hostile to your teaching.
- Don't let academic jargon like "resistance," "challenge," and "oppression" sanitize the truth of your teaching experiences. The real quotes of WFOC included here keep alive the harsh teaching realities that weigh heavily upon your shoulders.
- You have legitimate reasons to feel exhausted and overwhelmed by teaching. Dealing with classroom oppression requires you and WFOC to overexert three types of labor: Cognitive, affective, emotional. This overexertion has negative outcomes for you, your career outputs, and students.
- The SoTL is complicit in the maintenance of several teaching norms and myths that disproportionately and negatively affect WFOC.
- You and WFOC must make the suggested commitments of mind, heart, and action to make space, design, and build the teaching and academic futures you want and deserve. And yes, one is a commitment to the joyful sustenance that counter the atlas weight on your shoulders.

Empowering Actions You Can Take This Week

I did my part by dispelling the myths that might be obstacles to your teaching future. Now let's get to your part: Finish this chapter by luxuriating in your teaching and academic career fantasies and taking small steps towards it. Arrange a community of like-minded peers to do the same for support and accountability.

If you need baby steps before doing the strategic actions in the chapter, start with these:

1. Take a look at the quotes by WFOC about their teaching experiences and identify one that resonated deeply in your soul? How and/or why did that one speak to you?

2. Write your own quote to give voice (and validity) to your own inappropriately challenging/problematic and oppressive/ick/draining teaching experience(s).
3. Begin to reduce your teaching labor and replace it with restorative energy through these small actions:
   a. Identify at least one topic you can remove from your course to cut your teaching labor and increase student learning.
   b. Answer this question: What makes you feel successful or happy in the classroom?
   c. Find a low-stakes way to simply, joyfully, and easily add the above to at least one class session.
   d. Make a list of what you can do in fifteen minutes that might rejuvenate you, (re)fill your own cup, energize your body, feed your soul, or add joy to your day.
   e. Stop what you're doing right now and do one of the above. Go ahead. I'll wait.
4. Not sure how to do any one or all of the empowering actions above? Still resistant to reducing your teaching time, labor, and energy? Not sure how to put your own oxygen mask on first by rejuvenating and/or engaging in joy? Let's chat about it—reach out to me at empowered@effectivefaculty.org.

This is the most important chapter of this book as it maps a path to get you to the teaching future of your dreams, including retention, tenure, and promotion. You cannot persist in your role if you don't dial it back, replenish, and sustain yourself. You. Cannot. Persist. Ok? I'd love to hear about your journey to and arrival to a new teaching and academic reality filled with success and joy—so feel free to reach out to me with updates at empowered@effectivefaculty.org or www.empoweredacademic.org!

APPENDIX: FOR ALLIES

Here we are at the end of this book for women of color faculty. In it, I have done my level best to provide every opportunity for these women to improve their situation, to become empowered, to create joyful lives, and to continue to contribute. As one of these women, what I can say is, in addition to things I myself can do—over and above the things in the prior chapters that women of color faculty can do—there is another essential ingredient. To improve the lives of these women, that missing ingredient is you. You as a conscious, compassionate, and determined ally.

In the years that I've built my own teaching, mentoring, and consulting business in this arena, I'm sometimes approached with a conversation that's relevant. Here's the short version. Dr. Miller is obviously frustrated or pensive because they've newly (or long ago) become aware of teaching inequities for women faculty of color on campus. They tell me, "This seems insurmountable, what can I do?" I think, "JACKPOT!" and gleefully suggest ally actions. Now more than ever, we need more of this, so I'm glad you're one of the faculty, administrators, and developers who are transforming awareness into impactful action for women faculty of color.

Women faculty of color are not helpless, but they are living out their academic careers and their lives on a larger playing field, within a long-standing system of oppression and neglect. We can use every bit of friendship, support, and ally action we can get.

Because we can't change something this entrenched without everyone on board.

In addition to coming to grips with the rest of this book, here you'll find a checklist of actions for allies of all stripes. You can work through this on your own, as a department or unit, banding together with other allies in reading groups, faculty learning communities, communities of practice, and . . . *anywhere else you see women faculty of color whose teaching and academic career is at threat.*

Before diving in, let's lay out a working definition. What is an ally? What does allyship look like?

> Allyship is an ongoing, active and proactive commitment to the work of helping someone or a group of someones (with less privilege). It involves listening and responding rather than setting an agenda and imposing it.
>
> One type of ally is a white ally. A white ally acknowledges the limits of her/his/their knowledge about other people's experiences but doesn't use that as a reason not to think and/or act. A white ally does not remain silent.
>
> Being a white ally entails building relationships with both people of color, and also with white people in order to challenge them in their thinking about race. White allies don't have it all figured out, but are committed to non-complacency.[1]

With that working definition in mind, here are three categories of actions you can and should take as an ally, along with a visual reminder for each:

Categories and Levels of Action

Learn and Share: Micro-Change

These are things you do to increase your understanding and awareness so that you can better recognize the systematic teaching challenges facing women faculty of color (WFOC). This heightened awareness, however, is not as helpful when it

APPENDIX: FOR ALLIES   167

is insular. Therefore, it is essential that you also share that awareness with another colleague or administrator.

> Carefully read and digest this book is one example of a micro-change action.
>
> If you've read some of it and not yet shared, that is your next micro-change action.

On the levels of change, we can think of Learn and Share micro-actions as like adding sprinkles to an already existing cupcake. These are actions that enhance structural change.

Campus Culture Shifts: Meso-Change

In this category of action, make changes in your personal teaching practices because doing so will position those practices as normal and expected versus odd and suspicious. Also make changes in your conversations with colleagues and administrators to discuss those same teaching practices to further the culture shift of appreciating these less common practices as excellence instead of their current assessment of them as negative outliers.

> Integrate each chapter's described teaching practices into your own teaching—this is a good place to start with meso-change actions.
>
> Next, discuss your improved teaching practices and also your answers to the Empowering Actions section at the end of each chapter with colleagues and administrators to further a meso-level shift towards these teaching excellence practices.

For a visual for this level of ally action towards change, we can think of Culture Shift meso-actions as putting icing on an already existing cupcake. The icing is representative of moving structural changes into the living breathing reality of day-to-day life. Icing brings small cakes to life as cupcakes. Culture shifts bring structural changes to life.

Structural Foundational Necessities: Macro-Change

This third category of type of ally action is where you take actions that transform on an institutional level. These are the actions that produce the basic structural, resource, and policy features required for women faculty of color's survival on campuses. Reducing or eliminating unfair institutional obstacles is a prime example of a macro-level action that an ally like you should undertake.

> Propose, advocate for, and invest the labor to create the institutional structures, policies, and procedures that offset the major teaching threats to women faculty of color's academic careers as discussed in this book

To be clear, just because these actions make an impact on an institutional level, does not mean that one person cannot enact them. It is critical to note that one person is the ONLY thing that can kick-start institutional change, so use your authority, power, or influence to bring about institutional change, as this is where your help as an ally is most needed.

The cake—the structural foundation required for a cupcake—is the visual for this level of structural, institutional, and system change. In this case, your ally actions are used to transform a bunch of existing ingredients (e.g., current structures/policies/procedures) into something entirely new (e.g., new structures/policies/procedures). The icing (meso-level change) and sprinkles (micro-level change) cannot exist and are irrelevant without the cake itself. Your contributions towards creating the new reality of the cake are what makes the icing and sprinkles even possible. A fully baked cake, where the original ingredients have been transformed into something entirely new (and wonderful!) is the visual we use for structural foundational level change. Your ally contributions help create a new reality in the systems at your institution. All elements are working together and at their best.

Some Final Notes About the Categories and Levels of Action

There is no need to pick only one. In fact, the levels work well together–all three come together to produce a fantastic cupcake. Plan to take action from each category, and over time, you will find your unique strengths as an ally. You may wind up contributing more time in the cake category, or the icing category as you dig in; that's also exceedingly helpful.

Ally Actions to Take Now, In the Future, and Often

Now with the clarity the levels and categories bring, I am excited to see you bring your power, privileges, and passion to the table. The empowered campus is a campus where everyone wins, and your actions helping women faculty of color will be a win for everyone too. Recognize that some ally actions may feel easy and others difficult; the difficult parts are part of the journey of an ally, as well.

Now all that remains is for me to suggest ally actions from each category (and level). I encourage you to also go back and review the summaries from each chapter as needed.

Learn and Share Actions:

- Learn and Share the research on the exceptional teaching (e.g., goals, content, pedagogy) of women faculty of color and related benefits.
  - Make it clear to yourself and colleagues/administrators that different doesn't mean deficient, in this case it explicitly means exceptional and should be rewarded as such in retention/tenure/promotion reviews.

- Learn and Share the research on the resistance to WFOC's teaching—again not individual deficiency, rather a structural artifact.
  - Make the resistance WFOC face—that you may not be fully aware of—visible to yourself, colleagues, and administrators—along with a structural explanation of

resistance (not an individual WFOC faculty deficiency explanation) so this won't be held against them in reviews.

Campus Culture Shift Actions:

- Create and use a Classroom Behavior Expectations Statement exactly as described using the best practice guidance provided in Chapter 3.
    - For info on why it is important for allies to do so and why exactly as described, re-read the entire SoTL Minefield section in Chapter 3.

- Add (or add more) diverse or multiple perspectives to your course content to make doing so normative.
    - Don't gloss over this one. Make sure you aren't "diversifying" in the usual privileged way as illustrated in the examples in Chapter 4. Do it for REAL.

- Reflect upon a time when you or someone else might have silenced, discouraged, or punished the diverse or multiple perspectives course content of a WFOC.
    - To help you identify an instance, re-read Chapter 4.

Structural Foundation Necessities Actions:

- Push for training on the sound methodologically and quantitative ways to interpret student ratings (i.e., according to best practices for both quantitative and qualitative data analysis) when used in retention/tenure/promotion reviews.
    - "Many professional organizations have spoken out against using student ratings in reviews due to race and gender bias. Yet the people who conduct those reviews often have not been educated about how best to use them in evaluations. Training should focus on the ratings' benefits and limitations, their role among other methods of assessing teaching, the course and

APPENDIX: FOR ALLIES 171

professor features that may influence them, bias in student ratings, and proper data analysis. This training would be beneficial for all faculty members by providing the proper context for the effective use of ratings. And it should be required of faculty serving on tenure and promotion committees so that their practices are in line with the current research and guidance."[2]

- Eradicate current improper and Implement new sound practices, policies, and procedures to evaluate teaching for retention, tenure, and promotion.
  - "[WFOC] are disproportionately disadvantaged in reviews by the improper use of student evaluation and classroom observations. While most faculty handbooks describe different types of evidence for teaching effectiveness, most institutions give most (if not all) weight to student ratings. This runs counter to the evidence-based practice of reviewing teaching effectiveness by using multiple lenses and methods. Many institutions seem to cling to the student evaluations because that is how it has always been done and they are unsure how to do it differently. But if they want to retain [WFOC], institutions must establish an evidenced-based process to assess faculty's teaching effectiveness. And the time to do so is now."[3]

- Allocate resources for WFOC faculty to get teaching support off-campus (given the unique structural teaching challenges to their statuses) to support their reviews and academic success.
  - "reality is that, given the particular challenges they confront from institutional practices and processes, [WFOC] often need teaching support that might not be available on the campus. Institutions should provide course release time and money for [WFOC] to access off-campus conferences, workshops, training, coaches, consultants, mentors or teaching communities. This support is especially important on campuses without

a teaching and learning center or where the teaching center is already overloaded with other campus priorities (e.g., pandemic, AI, legislation) or has limited expertise and experience supporting [WFOC]."[4]

- Take an inventory of and adjust the teaching and advising assignments to reduce inequities/overloads for WFOC. In addition to the total number of courses, the distribution of new course preparations, service courses, and enrollment sizes should be examined, assessed, and adjusted. This more equitable load will allow the time and energy WFOC need to meet their research and grant expectations.
  - Easily start making teaching and advising workloads transparent using ideas from: KerryAnn O'Meara, Elizabeth Beise, Dawn Culpepper, Joya Misra, & Audrey Jaeger (2020) "Faculty Work Activity Dashboards: A Strategy to Increase Transparency," *Change: The Magazine of Higher Learning* 52, no. 3 (2020): 34–42.

At the end of this Appendix, and this book, I find myself with mixed feelings. Upon reflection, I realized it's very likely we are in the same boat. Do you have mixed feelings after absorbing the content and contemplating what you can do next as an ally?

I suppose by now you won't be surprised if I invite you to reflect on this, as I'll do here:

- I'm very excited to have all this information in one place so it can be referred to as and when needed on this journey towards empowered teaching and successful reviews for women of color faculty.
- I also feel sobered by how much work there is ahead. It's daunting, and I've been at this for over twenty years.
- I'm relieved that there will now be more of us equipped to talk about and get practices and structures in place for these issues. It's one thing to face challenges on one's own. And entirely another thing to have people to face them with at individual, interpersonal, and institutional levels.

- I'm hopeful that with a solid book in hand, it will be easier for change to happen. I look forward to pointing to my book and saying, "Read that!" and I deeply hope many people—allies included—will join me in that.

But most of all, my thoughts are with the women faculty of color this book has been written for and in support of. I know your journey has been long and you have been despairing yet determined. I'm sure reading this appendix has made it even clearer what your supporters, allies, and administrators should be doing to support your excellent and empowered teaching. There is a lot of road to travel, but if nothing else, through the actions listed above, your journey should be a little less lonely, better, and more successful.

How about you? How are you feeling after digesting the actions you can take next? Share them using #EmpoweredTeachingAlly on the social media platform of your preference so we can find one another. Have questions or just want more ally actions? Sure thing, reach out to me at www.empoweredacademic.org or empowered@effectivefaculty.org, I have plenty more ally actions to share!

Here's to you, ally. Thank you for reading and sharing this book far and wide. I'm so curious how you will put your power, privilege, and passion to work for the women of color faculty who are your colleagues, and what actions you will own from here.

ACKNOWLEDGMENTS

Quite a few years ago, I made a deal with myself as I pondered staying in or leaving academia. That deal? If I stayed, I'd spend even more time, energy, and labor ensuring that women of color—like me—are successful in higher education. I've lived up to that deal. My research, teaching, service, and consulting all support everything WFOC, and I'll continue to do so. But even though I spend so much of my working life bolstering WFOC to thrive within the system—I wanted to do even more. And that's how this book came about. I wrote it so that at any time, in any place, WFOC can have at their fingertips the strategies they need for career success. Period.

As I branched out in this way, I was reminded, and most of us probably agree, that academic writing sounds a certain kind of way. You know the tone. Usually formal and official sounding with big words and lengthy noun stacks in every paragraph. While that serves some purposes well, it absolutely wasn't a fit for this book. Nope. No matter how uncomfortable it felt at times or how it bucked academic conventions, I wanted to represent the seriousness of the topic, the magnitude and importance of this work and . . . write in my mentoring voice, the one you get when we're coaching or in a workshop together.

I also set a goal to make this as accessible and as action-oriented as possible, while of course meeting the criteria of the book publishers. Thank you to everyone at University of Oklahoma

Press for giving this much-needed title a home, in particular, series co-editor Michelle who really got my vision and answered all my newbie questions about how to make this book the best it could be.

Something I advocate for, but not as loudly as I could have in this book (ahem, book number two, perhaps?!) is how beautiful it is when a WFOC starts to thrive in her academic role, and as a result, the rest of her life begins to bloom. That's when things really start to synergize! Were it not for the nonacademic parts of my life, this book certainly would not be what it is. Time in nature camping with 'RD' the tomato plant, tumbleweed adventures every chance I got, reconnoitering breweries and communing with my 'boo' Lake Michigan, all contributed to my wholeness and the necessary energetic discharge to keep writing through all the ups and downs. Turns out, cross-country solo camping and writing first drafts of books DO go together!

Of course, a first draft has a long way to go before being in your hands, so a big thanks to early readers of *Empowered*. In the book writing process, I learned that early readers make an outsized difference to a manuscript, especially one that has ground-breaking and somewhat controversial components to it, and I had not one, but two sets of them. University of Oklahoma Press readers Jessamyn and Stacey, a deep thank you for "hearing" the book as I intended, as a "mentor-in-a-book" for women faculty of color. Your suggestions and feedback were invaluable! And to Zaire, Cynthia, Nao, Tasleem, Katy, and Kathryn, thanks for the generous input while things were still messy and unbaked. You all gave this book a big lift and extra oomph by affirming I was on to something writing about this topic—for us and to us!

My fellow faculty developers, including the WFOC in POD and elsewhere, Barbi, Kevin, Michelle, Katie, Tom, and Todd. Ya'll intently listened to my rants, which helped me sort out which gaps and issues should end up in this book.

People have started to ask me about the book writing process, so I want to say, embrace whatever helps you write! I credit the voice memo feature on my phone, which was a game-changer especially after being out in nature or doing some movement. Thank you to Andrea, my book coach, for going above and beyond and helping me hold firm to brazenly writing in my mentoring voice. And even though I now know how to avoid overdoing them, I still love a good noun stack and refuse to give them up entirely! Who knows what other adventures these new writing skills will bring?

In the end, I've discovered how much I enjoy writing scholarship in a personable and actionable way, even when it feels disharmonious with other people's ideas or is distinct from academic convention. Trusting my gut and expertise has been worth it. Writing this book has been difficult and took longer than I expected. But it has been worth it!

All joking about another book aside, who knows if there will be another, so I'm going to be thorough in my thanks.

My sands Carla, Ericka, Kathy, Toya, and Jan, you cheerleaded me all the way through, especially when I was sick and tired of writing, editing, and revising. And Rochelle, Marisha, and Erica, you never let me forget my why—success for women faculty of color, naturally—and told me I'm a bad mama jamma exactly when I needed to hear it.

Institutional clients, I send gratitude for our collaborations over 20 or more years, which inevitably informed these pages. I respect and admire your commitment to undoing unfair institutional barriers to WFOC, not always an easy commitment to keep. I'm hopeful and excited for the future successes of diverse faculty through your continued efforts and invite you to be in touch with your next project.

Big thanks to my mom and family for always being so proud and encouraging, no matter what I'm up to!

And of course . . . to each and every woman faculty of color:

THANK YOU for all of your fabulous contributions to higher education. Watching institutions ignore, penalize, or silence your brilliance is why I wrote this book. No more! This is it. I can't wait to see where you'll go with the data, tools, and ideas in this book. Let's do this.

Now all that remains is to place this book in the hands of every women of color faculty who will listen. If you've read this far, will you help make it so each and every one of us feels supported, encouraged, empowered, and proud . . . everything we deserve to feel but too rarely get on an institutional level? As I sign off, I imagine you saying a loud and resounding yes! For that, I acknowledge you here too. Thank you!

SUGGESTIONS FOR FURTHER RESOURCES
Want More? Start Here . . .

Wonderful women faculty of color—pat yourself on the back again for all the wonderful new knowledge and strategies you've gained by reading and using this book. You now know the intricacies of your teaching excellence, lurking structural obstacles to it, and what you can do to help protect you, your teaching, and your academic career. Bravo! I know your time and labor is already stretched thin, so trust that you have everything you need and don't need to do more. That said, if you'd like to learn more, go a bit deeper, or need a boost I make these two suggestions.

#1 Remain alert and empowered by making frequent visits to empoweredacademic.org

I'll keep this website updated with the most current and timely resources and readings since a lot of the relevant items for WFOC's teaching and well-being in their classrooms can change rather quickly (especially depending on what's currently going on in the world—I'm looking at you economic/political/social/environmental changes!)

#2 Boost your empowerment when necessary by drawing on a couple of these affirming/eye-opening/actionable sources of support

In addition to the book's website, you can check out the riches of support within the citations below to further bolster you and add additional empowerment on top of what you've already gotten out of the book.

AACU. "Essential Learning Outcomes." https://www.aacu.org/trending-topics/essential-learning-outcomes.

———. "How College Contributes to Workforce Success—Employer Views on What Matters Most." Washington, DC: Association of American Colleges and Universities, 2021. https://dgmg81phhvh63.cloudfront.net/content/user-photos/Research/PDFs/AACUEmployerReport2021.pdf.

Antonio, Anthony Lising. "Faculty of Color Reconsidered: Reassessing Contributions to Scholarship." *The Journal of Higher Education* 73, no. 5 (2002): 582–602.

Busteed, Brandon. "What's The Purpose Of College?" *Forbes,* April 10, 2019. https://www.forbes.com/sites/brandonbusteed/2019/04/10/whats-the-purpose-of-college/.

Castro, Corrine. "In the Margins of the Academy: Women of Color and Job Satisfaction." In *Dilemmas of Black Faculty at U.S. Predominantly White Institutions: Issues in the Post-Multicultural Era,* edited by S. E. Moore and R. Alexander Jr, 136–57. Edwin Mellen Press, 2010.

Domingo, Carmen R., Nancy Counts Gerber, Diane Harris, Laura Mamo, Sally G. Pasion, R. David Rebanal, and Sue V. Rosser. "More Service or More Advancement: Institutional Barriers to Academic Success for Women and Women of Color Faculty at a Large Public Comprehensive Minority-Serving State University." *Journal of Diversity in Higher Education*, 2020, 15(3), 365–79.

Griffin, Kimberly A. "Looking Beyond the Pipeline: Institutional Barriers, Strategies, and Benefits to Increasing the Representation of Women and Men of Color in the Professoriate." In *Higher Education: Handbook of Theory and Research,* edited by Laura Perna Vol. 35. Springer International, 2020, 1–73.

Gutiérrez, G. Muhs, Y. F. Niemann, C. G. González, and A. P. Harris. *Presumed Incompetent: The Intersections of Race and Class for Women in Academia*. Utah State University Press, 2012.

Harlow, Roxanna. "Race Doesn't Matter, but . . . : The Effect of Race on Professors' Experiences and Emotion Management in the Undergraduate College Classroom." *Social Psychology Quarterly* 66, no. 4 (2003): 348–63.

Lazos, S. "Are Student Teaching Evaluations Holding Back Women and Minorities: The Perils of Doing Gender and Race in the Classroom." In *Presumed Incompetent: The Intersections of Race and Class for Women in Academia*, edited by G. Gutierrez Y Muhs, Yolanda Flores Niemann, C. G. González, and A. P. Harris, 164–85. Utah State University Press, 2012.

Miller, Ryan A., Cathy D. Howell, and Laura Struve. "'Constantly, Excessively, and All the Time': The Emotional Labor of Teaching Diversity Courses." *International Journal of Teaching and Learning in Higher Education* 31, no. 3 (2019): 491–502.

Misra, Joya, Alexandra Kuvaeva, Kerryann O'Meara, Dawn Kiyoe Culpepper, and Audrey Jaeger. "Gendered and Racialized Perceptions of Faculty Workloads." *Gender & Society* 35, no. 3 (2021): 358–94.

Nilson, Linda B. *Teaching at Its Best: A Research-Based Resource for College Instructor.* John Wiley & Sons, 2016.

O'Meara, Kerryann, Dawn Culpepper, Joya Misra, and Audrey Jaeger. "Equity-Minded Faculty Workloads: What We Can and Should Do Now." Washington, D.C.: American Council on Education, 2022. https://www.acenet.edu/Documents/Equity-Minded-Faculty-Workloads.pdf.

Pittman, Chavella T. "Colleges Must Change to Retain BIPOC Women Faculty." *Inside Higher Ed,* April 30, 2021. https://www.insidehighered.com/advice/2021/04/30/retain-bipoc-women-faculty-colleges-must-remove-obstacles-they-face-opinion.

———. "Keys to Unlocking Tenure and Academic Freedom". *AAUP Blog*, March 7, 2023, https://academeblog.org/2023/03/07/keys-to-unlocking-tenure-and-academic-freedom/.

———. "Race and Gender Oppression in the Classroom: The Experiences of Women Faculty of Color with White Male Students." *Teaching Sociology* 38, no. 3 (July 1, 2010): 183–96.

———. "The Overlooked Minefield." *Inside Higher Ed*, April 15, 2021. https://www.insidehighered.com/advice/2021/04/16/teaching-issues-can-be-among-biggest-obstacles-retaining-bipoc-women-faculty.

Stolzenberg, Ellen Bara, M. Kevin Eagan Jr., Hilary B. Zimmerman, Jennifer Berdan Lozano, Natacha M. Cesar-Davis, Melissa C. Aragon, and Cecilia Rios-Aguilar. "Undergraduate Teaching Faculty: The HERI Faculty Survey 2016–2017." Higher Education Research Institute: UCLA, 2019.

Turner, Caroline Sotello Viernes. "Women of Color in Academe." *Journal of Higher Education* 73, no. 1 (February 1, 2002): 74–93.

Umbach, P. D. "The Contribution of Faculty of Color to Undergraduate Education." *Research in Higher Education* 47, no. 3 (2006): 317–45.

Wells, J. B., and L. K. Crain. "Council for the Advancement of Standards in High Education (2023)." CAS Learning and Development Outcomes, CAS Professional Standards for Higher Education (Version 11), 2023. https://www.cas.edu/student-learning—development-outcomes.html.

Zambrana, Ruth E. *Toxic Ivory Towers: The Health Consequences of Work Stress on the Health of Underrepresented Minority Faculty.* Rutgers University Press, 2018.

Zambrana, Ruth. E., R. Burciaga Valdez, Chavella T. Pittman, Todd Bartko, Lynn Weber, and Deborah Parra-Medina. "Workplace Stress and Discrimination Effects on the Physical and Depressive Symptoms of Underrepresented Minority Faculty." *Stress and Health : Journal of the International Society for the Investigation of Stress* 37, no. 1 (2021): 175–85. https://doi.org/10.1002/smi.2983.

NOTES

Introduction

1. Are you reading this but aren't a woman faculty of color, yet have marginalized statuses? Welcome, and do keep reading. I wouldn't do any of us the disservice of describing diverse faculty monolithically, and of course we all navigate our own complicated intersectional matrix of statuses—but odds are the strategies in this book are relevant for your teaching and renewal, tenure, and promotion reviews. I hope you find it as actionable as I intend it.

Don't belong to a marginalized group? Pay attention. You won't be centered here, but there is MUCH you'll learn about teaching threats to WFOC and more importantly the ally actions you can take, particularly those in the appendix. I and my fellow WFOC call on you to actively support our humanity, teaching, and career success.

Chapter 1

1. The names in the stories of WFOC's experiences in this book are pseudonyms—some are specific cases, composites, or illustrations. I intermingled these types as much as possible to keep them protected and unidentifiable.

2. Kimberly A. Griffin, "Looking Beyond the Pipeline: Institutional Barriers, Strategies, and Benefits to Increasing the Representation of Women and Men of Color in the Professoriate," in *Higher Education: Handbook of Theory and Research*, ed. Laura W. Perna, 35 (Springer

International, 2020): 1–73; Chavella T. Pittman, "Evaluating the Teaching Effectiveness of Black Women Faculty," *Journal of Negro Education* 90, no. 4 (2021): 442–56; Ellen Bara Stolzenberg et al., "Undergraduate Teaching Faculty: The HERI Faculty Survey 2016–2017" (Higher Education Research Institute: UCLA, 2019).

3. C. Turner, J. C. Gonzalez, and J. Wood, "Faculty of Color in Academe: What 20 Years of Literature Tells Us," *Journal of Diversity in Higher Education* 1, no. 3 (2008): 139–68.

4. A. L. Antonio, "Faculty of Color Reconsidered: Reassessing Contributions to Scholarship," *The Journal of Higher Education* 73, no. 5 (2002): 582–602; S. Freeman et al., "Active Learning Increases Student Performance in Science, Engineering, and Mathematics," *Proceedings of the National Academy of Sciences* 111, no. 23 (2014): 8410–15, https://doi.org/10.1073/pnas.1319030111; M. F. Knowles and B. W. Harleston, *Achieving Diversity in the Professorate: Challenges and Opportunities* (American Council on Education, 1997); G. Kuh, K. O'Donnell, and C. Schneider, "HIPs at Ten," *Change* 49, no. 5 (2017): 8–16; M. Prince, "Does Active Learning Work? A Review of the Research," *Journal of Engineering Education* 93, no. 3 (2004): 223–31, https://doi.org/10.1002/j.2168-9830.2004.tb00809.x; Turner, Gonzalez, and Wood, "Faculty of Color in Academe: What 20 Years of Literature Tells Us"; P. D. Umbach, "The Contribution of Faculty of Color to Undergraduate Education," *Research in Higher Education* 47, no. 3 (2006): 317–45; Rashné R Jehangir, "Stories as Knowledge: Bringing the Lived Experience of First-Generation College Students Into the Academy," *Urban Education* 45, no. 4 (2010): 533–53.

5. Griffin, "Looking Beyond the Pipeline."

6. Antonio, "Faculty of Color Reconsidered"; Umbach, "The Contribution of Faculty of Color to Undergraduate Education."

7. Antonio, "Faculty of Color Reconsidered"; Stolzenberg et al., "Undergraduate Teaching Faculty."

8. Umbach, "The Contribution of Faculty of Color to Undergraduate Education"; Patricia Hill Collins, *Black Feminist Thought: Knowledge, Consciousness, and the Politics of Empowerment* (Routledge, 2002); bell hooks, *Teaching Critical Thinking: Practical Wisdom* (Routledge, 2010).

9. Antonio Gramsci, *Prison Notebooks*, vols. 1–3, trans. and ed. Joseph A. Buttigieg and Antonio Callari (Columbia University Press, 2011); Marcia B. Baxter Magolda, "Teaching to Promote Holistic Learning and Development," *New Directions for Teaching and Learning* 2000, no. 82 (2000): 88–98, https://doi.org/10.1002/tl.8209; O. Villalpando and D. Delgado, "A Critical Race Theory Analysis of Barriers That

Impede the Success of Faculty of Color," in *The Racial Crisis in American Higher Education: Continuing Challenges for the Twenty-First Century*, ed. W. A. Smith, P. G. Altbach, and K. Lomotey (State University of New York Press, 2002), 243–69; Lisa E. Wolf-Wendel and Marti Ruel, "Developing the Whole Student: The Collegiate Ideal," *New Directions for Higher Education*, 1999, no. 105 (1999): 35–46, https://doi.org/10.1002/he.10503.

10. Antonio, "Faculty of Color Reconsidered"; Villalpando and Delgado, "A Critical Race Theory Analysis of Barriers That Impede the Success of Faculty of Color."

11. Collins, *Black Feminist Thought*; hooks, *Teaching Critical Thinking*.

12. E.g., D. Hassouneh, "Anti-Racist Pedagogy: Challenges Faced by Faculty of Color in Predominantly White Schools of Nursing," *Journal of Nursing Education* 45, no. 7 (2006): 255–63; Olivia Perlow, D Wheeler, and Sharon Bethea, "Dismantling the Master's House: Black Women Faculty Challenging White Privilege/Supremacy in the College Classroom," *White Privilege Conference Journal* 42, no. 2 (2014): 251–59; Villalpando and Delgado, "A Critical Race Theory Analysis of Barriers That Impede the Success of Faculty of Color."

13. Carmen R. Domingo et al., "More Service or More Advancement: Institutional Barriers to Academic Success for Women and Women of Color Faculty at a Large Public Comprehensive Minority-Serving State University," *Journal of Diversity in Higher Education* 15, no. 3 (2022): 365–79; KerryAnn O'Meara, Alexandra Kuvaeva, and Gudrun Nyunt, "Constrained Choices: A View of Campus Service Inequality from Annual Faculty Reports," *The Journal of Higher Education* 88, no. 5 (2017): 672–700; Joya Misra et al., "Gendered and Racialized Perceptions of Faculty Workloads," *Gender & Society* 35, no. 3 (2021): 358–94.

14. Walter R. Allen et al., "Outsiders within: Race, Gender, and Faculty Status in U. S. Higher Education," in *The Racial Crisis in American Higher Education: Continuing Challenges for the Twenty-First Century*, ed. W. A. Smith, P. G. Altbach, and K. Lomotey (SUNY University Press, 2002): 189–220; Villalpando and Delgado, "A Critical Race Theory Analysis of Barriers That Impede the Success of Faculty of Color"; Ryan A. Miller, Cathy D. Howell, and Laura Struve, "'Constantly, Excessively, and All the Time': The Emotional Labor of Teaching Diversity Courses," *International Journal of Teaching and Learning in Higher Education* 31, no. 3 (2019): 491–502.

15. Jehangir, "Stories as Knowledge."

16. Sylvia Hurtado and Adrian Ruiz Alvarado, "Discrimination and Bias, Underrepresentation, and Sense of Belonging on Campus"

(Higher Education Research Institute, 2015); Terrell L. Strayhorn, *College Students' Sense of Belonging: A Key to Educational Success for All Students*, 2nd ed. (New York, 2019).

17. Antonio, "Faculty of Color Reconsidered"; Griffin, "Looking Beyond the Pipeline"; Paul D. Umbach, "The Contribution of Faculty of Color to Undergraduate Education," *Research in Higher Education* 47, no. 3 (May 1, 2006): 317–45, https://doi.org/10.1007/s11162-005-9391-3.

18. S. Lazos, "Are Student Teaching Evaluations Holding Back Women and Minorities: The Perils of Doing Gender and Race in the Classroom," in *Presumed Incompetent: The Intersections of Race and Class for Women in Academia*, ed. G. Gutiérrez et al. (Utah State University Press, 2012), 164–85; P. A. Matthew, ed., *Written/Unwritten: Diversity and the Hidden Truths of Tenure* (University of North California Press, 2016).

19. Gutiérrez et al., *Presumed Incompetent: The Intersections of Race and Class for Women in Academia* (Utah State University Press, 2012); Chavella T. Pittman, "Race and Gender Oppression in the Classroom: The Experiences of Women Faculty of Color with White Male Students," *Teaching Sociology* 38, no. 3 (July 1, 2010): 183–96; Miller, Howell, and Struve, "'Constantly, Excessively, and All the Time'."

20. Pittman, "Race and Gender Oppression in the Classroom."

21. K. A. Griffin, "Redoubling Our Efforts: How Institutions Can Affect Faculty Diversity," *Race and Ethnicity in Higher Education* (February 14, 2019) American Council on Education. (2019, February 14), https://www.equityinhighered.org/resources/ideas-and-insights/redoubling-our-efforts-how-institutions-can-affect-faculty-diversity/; R. E. Zambrana, A. Harvey Wingfield, L.M. Lapeyrouse, B. A. Dávila, T. L. Hoagland, and R. B. Valdez, "Blatant, Subtle, and Insidious: URM Faculty Perceptions of Discriminatory Practices in Predominantly White Institutions," *Sociological Inquiry*, 87, no. 2 (2017): 207–232; KerryAnn O'Meara, Lindsey Templeton, and Gudrun Nyunt, "Earning Professional Legitimacy: Challenges Faced by Women, Underrepresented Minority, and Non-Tenure-Track Faculty," *Teachers College Record*, 120 (2018): 1–38.

22. Pittman, "Race and Gender Oppression in the Classroom."

23. Diana B. Kardia and Mary C. Wright, "Instructor Identity: The Impact of Gender and Race on Faculty Experiences with Teaching," *CRLT, Occasional Papers* 19 (2004).

24. I. H. Settles, M. K. Jones, N. T. Buchanan, & S. T. Brassel, "Epistemic Exclusion of Women Faculty and Faculty of Color: Understanding Scholar(ly) Devaluation as a Predictor of Turnover Intentions." *The*

Journal of Higher Education, 93, no. 1 (2021): 31–55; D. Kozlowski, V. Larivière, C. R. Sugimoto, & T. Monroe-White, "Intersectional inequalities in science," *Proceedings of the National Academy of Sciences. USA* 119, e2113067119 (2022); David Folkenflik, "UNC Journalism School Tried To Give Nikole Hannah-Jones Tenure. A Top Donor Objected" (June 21, 2021) *NPR*, https://www.npr.org/2021/06/21/1007778651/journalism-race-and-the-fight-over-nikole-hannah-jones-tenure-at-unc; R. E. Zambrana, A. Harvey Wingfield, L.M. Lapeyrouse, B. A. Dávila, T. L. Hoagland, and R. B. Valdez, "Blatant, Subtle, and Insidious: URM Faculty Perceptions of Discriminatory Practices in Predominantly White Institutions," *Sociological Inquiry*, 87, no. 2 (2017): 207–232.

25. Saida Grundy, "A History of White Violence Tells Us Attacks on Black Academics Are Not Ending (I Know Because It Happened to Me)," *Ethnic and Racial Studies* 40, no. 11 (September 2017): 1864–71.

26. Roxanna Harlow, "Race Doesn't Matter, but . . . : The Effect of Race on Professors' Experiences and Emotion Management in the Undergraduate College Classroom," *Social Psychology Quarterly* 66, no. 4 (2003): 348–63; Robert Kevin Toutkoushian and Marcia L. Bellas, "Faculty Time Allocations and Research Productivity: Gender, Race and Family Effects," *The Review of Higher Education* 22, no. 4 (1999): 367–90; Misra et al., "Gendered and Racialized Perceptions of Faculty Workloads."

27. Talisa J. Carter and Craig O. Miltonette, "It Could Be Us: Black Faculty as 'Threats' on the Path to Tenure," *Race and Justice* 12, no. 3 (2022): 569–587.

28. Lazos, "Are Student Teaching Evaluations Holding Back Women and Minorities"; Uma A. Jayakumar et al., "Racial Privilege in the Professoriate: An Exploration of Campus Climate, Retention, and Satisfaction," *The Journal of Higher Education* 80, no. 5 (2009): 538–63.

29. Harlow, "Race Doesn't Matter, but . . ."

30. Roxanna Zambrana, *Toxic Ivory Towers: The Health Consequences of Work Stress on the Health of Underrepresented Minority Faculty* (Rutgers University Press, 2018); Ruth E. Zambrana et al., "Workplace Stress and Discrimination Effects on the Physical and Depressive Symptoms of Underrepresented Minority Faculty," *Stress and Health: Journal of the International Society for the Investigation of Stress* 37, no. 1 (2021): 175–85, https://doi.org/10.1002/smi.2983; C. Castro, "In the Margins of the Academy: Women of Color and Job Satisfaction," in *Dilemmas of Black Faculty at U.S. Predominantly White Institutions: Issues in the Post-Multicultural Era*, ed. S. E. Moore and R. Alexander Jr. (Edwin Mellen Press, 2010), 136–57.

31. Again, I am using a pseudonym to protect this woman of color academic although she did give me permission to use both her name and the public letter she has posted.

32. Oxford University Press Dictionary, "S.v. 'Keystone,'" accessed August 13, 2022, https://languages.oup.com/google-dictionary-en/.

33. Peter Seldin, *Successful Use of Teaching Portfolios* (Anker Pub. Co, 1993); Peter Seldin, *The Teaching Portfolio: A Practical Guide to Improved Performance and Promotion/Tenure Decisions*, 3rd ed. (Anker Publishing Company, 2004), https://cft.vanderbilt.edu/guides-sub-pages/teaching-portfolios/; Joe T. Davis and Louis J. Swift, "Teaching Portfolios at a Research University," *Louis Journal on Excellence in College Teaching* 6, no. 1 (1995): 101–15.

34. Susan A. Ambrose et al., eds., *How Learning Works: Seven Research-Based Principles for Smart Teaching*, 1st ed., The Jossey-Bass Higher and Adult Education Series (Jossey-Bass, 2010); Nancy Chism, "Developing a Philosophy of Teaching Statement" in *Essays on Teaching Excellence Toward the Best in the Academy*, 9, no. 3 (1997–98), http://podnetwork.org/content/uploads/V9-N3-Chism.pdf; Dieter J. Schönwetter et al., "Teaching Philosophies Reconsidered: A Conceptual Model for the Development and Evaluation of Teaching Philosophy Statements," *International Journal for Academic Development* 7, no. 1 (2002): 83–97; Mary-Ann Winkelmes et al., "A Teaching Intervention That Increases Underserved College Students' Success," *Peer Review* 18 Winter/Spring, no. 1/2 (2016): 31–36.

35. Some, many, or most of us teach in contexts with legislative or other explicit threats to academic freedom. Nothing will make you invulnerable. However, the academic freedom that institutions profess for faculty will still give you and your allies something to hold on to, to protect your career. Women faculty of color are the canaries in the coal mine. They are the early warning system to threats to academic freedom for EVERYONE. Read this piece to learn more about why everyone–colleagues, institutions, and organizations–should be alarmed when WFOC face threats to their academic freedom: https://academeblog.org/2023/03/07/keys-to-unlocking-tenure-and-academic-freedom/

36. American Association of University Professors, "FAQs on Academic Freedom," n.d., https://www.aaup.org/programs/academic-freedom/faqs-academic-freedom, accessed June 19, 2023.

37. Judith L. Pace and Annette Hemmings, "Understanding Authority in Classrooms: A Review of Theory, Ideology, and Research," *Review of Educational Research* 77, no. 1 (2007): 4–27.

Chapter 2

1. A. Aguirre, "Women and Minority Faculty in the Academic Workplace: Recruitment, Retention, and Academic Culture," *ASHE-ERIC Higher Education Report* 27, no. 6 (2000), https://eric.ed.gov/?id=ED447752; Bryan McKinley Jones Brayboy, "The Implementation of Diversity in Predominantly White Colleges and Universities," *Journal of Black Studies* 34, no. 1 (September 1, 2003): 72–86, https://doi.org/10.1177/0021934703253679; Catherine Medina and Gaye Luna, "Narratives from Latina Professors in Higher Education," *Anthropology & Education Quarterly* 31, no. 1 (March 1, 2000): 47–66; Yolanda T. Moses, "Black Women in the Academy: Promises and Perils," in *Black Women in the Academy: Promises and Perils*, ed. Lois Benjamin, 1st ed. (University Press of Florida, 1997), 23–38; Caroline Sotello Viernes Turner, "Women of Color in Academe: Living with Multiple Marginality," *The Journal of Higher Education* 73, no. 1 (2001): 74–93.

2. Sekile M. Nzinga-Johnson, *Lean Semesters: How Higher Education Reproduces Inequity*, Critical University Studies (Johns Hopkins University Press, 2020).

3. Emma Whitford, "There Are So Few That Have Made Their Way," *Inside Higher Education*, October 27, 2020, https://www.insidehighered.com/news/2020/10/28/black-administrators-are-too-rare-top-ranks-higher-education-it%E2%80%99s-not-just-pipeline.

4. Walter R. Allen et al., "Outsiders within: Race, Gender, and Faculty Status in U. S. Higher Education," in *The Racial Crisis in American Higher Education: Continuing Challenges for the Twenty-First Century*, ed. W. A. Smith, P. G. Altbach, and K. Lomotey (SUNY University Press, 2002): 189–220; Benjamin Baez, "Negotiating and Resisting Racism: How Faculty of Color Construct Promotion and Tenure," Eric Document Report No. 430-420. Retrieved January 12, 2008, from https://files.eric.ed.gov/fulltext/ED430420.pdf; Elizabeth G. Creamer, "Assessing Faculty Publication Productivity: Issues of Equity" (ERIC Clearinghouse on Higher Education, Institute for Education Policy Studies, Graduate School of Education and Human Development, the George Washington University, 1998); Sheila T. Gregory, "Black Faculty Women in the Academy: History, Status, and Future," *Journal of Negro Education* 70, no. 3 (Summer 2001): 124–38, https://doi.org/10.2307/3211205; O. Villalpando and D. Delgado, "A Critical Race Theory Analysis of Barriers That Impede the Success of Faculty of Color," in *The Racial Crisis in American Higher Education: Continuing Challenges for the Twenty-First*

Century, ed. W. A. Smith, P. G. Altbach, and K. Lomotey (State University of New York Press, 2002), 243–69; Moses, "Black Women in the Academy."

5. Social Sciences Feminist Network Research Interest Group, "The Burden of Invisible Work in Academia: Social Inequalities and Time Use in Five University Departments," *Humboldt Journal of Social Relations* 39 (2017): 228–45.

6. Brandon Busteed, "What's The Purpose Of College?," *Forbes*, April 10, 2019.

7. AACU, "How College Contributes to Workforce Success—Employer Views on What Matters Most" (Association of American Colleges and Universities, n.d.); J. B. Wells and L. K. Crain, "Council for the Advancement of Standards in High Education (2023)," CAS Learning and Development Outcomes, CAS Professional Standards for Higher Education (Version 11), 2023; Kim Dancy, Genevieve Garcia-Kendrick, and Diane Cheng, "Rising above the Threshold: How Expansions in Financial Aid Can Increase the Equitable Delivery of Postsecondary Value for More Students" (Institution of Higher Education Policy, June 2023), https://www.ihep.org/wp-content/uploads/2023/06/IHEP_Rising-above-the-Threshold_rd4.pdf.

8. AACU, "Essential Learning Outcomes," accessed March 2, 2022, https://www.aacu.org/trending-topics/essential-learning-outcomes; Anthony Lising Antonio, "Faculty of Color Reconsidered: Reassessing Contributions to Scholarship," *Journal of Higher Education* 73, no. 5 (2002): 582–602; Aguirre, *Women and Minority Faculty in the Academic Workplace*; Olivia Perlow, Durene Wheeler, and Sharon Bethea, "Dismantling the Master's House: Black Women Faculty Challenging White Privilege/Supremacy in the College Classroom," *White Privilege Conference Journal* 4, no. 2 (2014): 241–59.

9. Antonio, "Faculty of Color Reconsidered"; Dena Hassouneh, "Anti-Racist Pedagogy: Challenges Faced by Faculty of Color in Predominantly White Schools of Nursing," *Journal of Nursing Education* 45, no. 7 (July 2006): 255–62; Perlow, Wheeler, and Bethea, "Dismantling the Master's House"; Octavio Villalpando, "The Impact of Diversity and Multiculturalism on All Students: Findings from a National Study," *NASPA Journal* 40, no. 1 (November 1, 2002): 124–44, https://doi.org/10.2202/1949-6605.1194.

10. Ellen Bara Stolzenberg et al., "Undergraduate Teaching Faculty: The HERI Faculty Survey 2016–2017" (Higher Education Research Institute: UCLA, 2019); Rhonesha Byng, "Failure Is Not An Option: The

Pressure Black Women Feel To Succeed," *Forbes*, August 31, 2017; Greta Anderson, "Front and Center," *Inside Higher Ed*, November 23, 2020; Tanya A. Christian, "Black Women's Equal Pay Day Puts Workforce Progression into Questions," *Ebony*, September 21, 2022.

11. Antonio, "Faculty of Color Reconsidered"; Kimberly A. Griffin, "Looking Beyond the Pipeline: Institutional Barriers, Strategies, and Benefits to Increasing the Representation of Women and Men of Color in the Professoriate," in *Higher Education: Handbook of Theory and Research*, ed. Laura W. Perna, 35 (Springer International, 2020): 1–73.

12. P. D. Umbach, "The Contribution of Faculty of Color to Undergraduate Education," *Research in Higher Education* 47, no. 3 (2006): 317–45.

13. Roy Y. Chan, "Understanding the Purpose of Higher Education: An Analysis of the Economic and Social Benefits for Completing a College Degree," *Journal of Education Policy, Planning and Administration (JEPPA)* 65 (2016): 1–40.

14. AACU, "Essential Learning Outcomes."

15. AACU, "Essential Learning Outcomes," Trending Topic, accessed March 3, 2022, https://www.aacu.org/trending-topics/e.

16. Griffin, "Looking Beyond the Pipeline."

17. AACU, "Essential Learning Outcomes."

18. Griffin, "Looking Beyond the Pipeline"; Paul D. Umbach, "The Contribution of Faculty of Color to Undergraduate Education," *Research in Higher Education* 47, no. 3 (May 1, 2006): 317–45, https://doi.org/10.1007/s11162-005-9391-3; Antonio, "Faculty of Color Reconsidered."

19. Stolzenberg et al., "Undergraduate Teaching Faculty"; Perlow, Wheeler, and Bethea, "Dismantling the Master's House."

20. Griffin, "Looking Beyond the Pipeline."

21. AACU, "Essential Learning Outcomes."

22. Griffin, "Looking Beyond the Pipeline."

23. AACU, "Essential Learning Outcomes."

24. Griffin, "Looking Beyond the Pipeline."

25. Griffin, "Looking Beyond the Pipeline."

26. AACU, "Essential Learning Outcomes."

27. Griffin, "Looking Beyond the Pipeline."

28. Wells and Crain, "Council for the Advancement of Standards in High Education (2023)."

29. AACU, "Essential Learning Outcomes."

30. AACU, "Essential Learning Outcomes."

31. AACU, "Essential Learning Outcomes."

32. AACU, "Essential Learning Outcomes."

33. Stuart Hall, "Gramsci's Relevance for the Study of Race and Ethnicity," *Journal of Communication Inquiry* 10, no. 2 (1986): 5–27; Antonio Gramsci, *Prison Notebooks*, edited and translated by Joseph A. Buttigieg with Antonio Callari, vols. 1, 2, 3 (Columbia University Press, 2011).

34. Devah Pager and Hana Shepherd, "The Sociology of Discrimination: Racial Discrimination in Employment, Housing, Credit, and Consumer Markets," *Annual Review of Sociology* 34, no. 1 (August 2008): 181–209; Darreonna Davis, "Black Women Are Less Likely To Get Quality Feedback At Work. That Impacts Their Earnings And Leadership Opportunities Over Time," *Forbes*, 2022, https://www.forbes.com/sites/darreonnadavis/2022/06/15/black-women-are-less-likely-to-get-quality-feedback-at-work-that-impacts-their-earnings-and-leadership-opportunities-over-time/?sh=563a28f67b7a; Joan C. Williams et al., "How One Company Worked to Root Out Bias from Performance Reviews," *Harvard Business Review*, April 21, 2021; Hall, "Gramsci's Relevance for the Study of Race and Ethnicity"; Shelley J. Correll et al., "Inside the Black Box of Organizational Life: The Gendered Language of Performance Assessment," *American Sociological Review* 85, no. 6 (2020): 1022–50.

35. Yolanda Flores Niemann, Gabriella Gutiérrez y Muhs, and Carmen G. Gonzalez, eds., *Presumed Incompetent II: Race, Class, Power, and Resistance of Women in Academia* (Utah State University Press, 2020); Chavella T. Pittman, "The Overlooked Minefield," *Inside Higher Ed*, April 15, 2021.

36. Griffin, "Looking Beyond the Pipeline"; Antonio, "Faculty of Color Reconsidered"; Perlow, Wheeler, and Bethea, "Dismantling the Master's House"; Umbach, "The Contribution of Faculty of Color to Undergraduate Education."

37. AACU, "Essential Learning Outcomes."

38. AACU, "Essential Learning Outcomes."

39. ALA, "Framework for Information Literacy for Higher Education," American Library Association, February 9, 2015, https://www.ala.org/acrl/standards/ilframework; International Federation of Library Associations and Institutions, "Beacons of the Information Society: The Alexandria Proclamation on Information Literacy and Lifelong Learning," UNESCO, 2005, https://www.ifla.org/publications/beacons-of-the-information-society-the-alexandria-proclamation-on-information-literacy-and-lifelong-learning/.

40. AACU, "How College Contributes to Workforce Success."

41. AACU, "Essential Learning Outcomes."

42. AACU, "Essential Learning Outcomes."

43. Dalia Rodriguez et al., "Practicing Liberatory Pedagogy: Women of Color in College Classrooms," *Cultural Studies ↔ Critical Methodologies* 12, no. 2 (2012): 96–108; Griffin, "Looking Beyond the Pipeline"; Niemann, Gutiérrez y Muhs, and Gonzalez, *Presumed Incompetent II*.

44. Griffin, "Looking Beyond the Pipeline"; Chavella T. Pittman, "Evaluating the Teaching Effectiveness of Black Women Faculty," *Journal of Negro Education* 90, no. 4 (2021): 442–56; Ruth E. Zambrana et al., "Workplace Stress and Discrimination Effects on the Physical and Depressive Symptoms of Underrepresented Minority Faculty," *Stress and Health: Journal of the International Society for the Investigation of Stress* 37, no. 1 (2021): 175–85, https://doi.org/10.1002/smi.2983.

45. Stolzenberg et al., "Undergraduate Teaching Faculty."

46. AACU, "Essential Learning Outcomes"; Wells and Crain, "Council for the Advancement of Standards in High Education (2023)."

47. Gutierrez y Muhs, *Presumed Incompetent: The Intersections of Race and Class for Women in Academia* (University Press of Colorado, 2012); Niemann, Gutiérrez y Muhs, and Gonzalez, *Presumed Incompetent II*.

48. TaLisa J. Carter and Miltonette O. Craig, "It Could Be Us: Black Faculty as 'Threats' on the Path to Tenure," *Race and Justice* 12, no. 3 (2022): 569–87; Griffin, "Looking Beyond the Pipeline"; Pittman, "The Overlooked Minefield."

Chapter 3

1. David Ginsburg, "Behavior Management ≠ Classroom Management," *Education Week*, April 3, 2011, sec. Teaching, https://www.edweek.org/teaching-learning/opinion-behavior-management-classroom-management/2011/04.

2. Kerryann O'Meara et al., "Equity-Minded Faculty Workloads: What We Can and Should Do Now" (American Council on Education, 2022); Kimberly A. Griffin, "Looking Beyond the Pipeline: Institutional Barriers, Strategies, and Benefits to Increasing the Representation of Women and Men of Color in the Professoriate," in *Higher Education: Handbook of Theory and Research*, ed. Laura W. Perna, 35 (Springer International, 2020): 1–73.

3. Linda B. Nilson, *Teaching at Its Best: A Research-Based Resource for College Instructors*, 3rd ed. (Jossey-Bass, 2010).

4. Sharon Bart, "Classroom Management Tips for New College Instructors, Faculty Focus," Higher Ed Teaching Strategies from Magna Publications, 2008, https://www.facultyfocus.com/articles/effective-classroom-management/15-survival-strategies-for-new-college-instructors-2/.

5. Nilson, *Teaching at Its Best*.

6. Margaret C. Wang, Geneva D. Haertel, and Herbert J. Walberg, "Toward a Knowledge Base for School Learning," *Review of Educational Research* 63, no. 3 (1993): 249–94.

7. Robert J. Marzano and Jana S. Marzano, "The Key to Classroom Management," *Educational Leadership* 61, no. 1 (2003): 6–13.

8. Roxanna Harlow, "Race Doesn't Matter, but . . . : The Effect of Race on Professors' Experiences and Emotion Management in the Undergraduate College Classroom," *Social Psychology Quarterly* 66, no. 4 (December 2003): 348–63; J. M. McGowan, "Multicultural Teaching: African-American Faculty Classroom Teaching Experiences in Predominantly White Colleges and Universities," *Multicultural Education* 8, no. 2 (2000): 19–22; V. A. Moore, "Inappropriate Challenges to Professional Authority," *Teaching Sociology* 24 (1996): 202–06; Chavella T. Pittman, "Race and Gender Oppression in the Classroom: The Experiences of Women Faculty of Color with White Male Students," *Teaching Sociology* 38, no. 3 (July 1, 2010): 183–96; C. Pittman, *Incivility in the Classroom: Effective Strategies for Faculty at the Margins in Difficult Subjects: Insights and Strategies for Teaching Race, Sexuality and Gender* (Stylus Publishing, 2018); Elizabeth A. Taylor, Robin Hardin Taylor, and Cheryl R. Rode, "Contrapower Harassment in the Sport Management Classroom," *NASPA Journal About Women in Higher Education* 11, no. 1 (2017): 17–32.

9. Dave A. Louis et al., "Afro-Caribbean Immigrant Faculty Experiences in the American Academy: Voices of an Invisible Black Population," *The Urban Review* 49, no. 4 (2017): 668–91.

10. D. B. Kardia and M. Wright, "Instructor Identity: The Impact of Gender and Race on Faculty Experiences with Teaching" (University of Michigan Center for Research on Learning and Teaching, 2004).

11. Lucila Vargas, "When the 'Other' Is the Teacher: Implications of Teacher Diversity in Higher Education," *The Urban Review* 31, no. 4 (1999): 371.

12. Roxanna Harlow, "Race Doesn't Matter, but . . . : The Effect of Race on Professors' Experiences and Emotion Management in the Undergraduate College Classroom," *Social Psychology Quarterly* 66, no. 4

(2003): 348–63; Louis et al., "Afro-Caribbean Immigrant Faculty Experiences in the American Academy"; McGowan, "Multicultural Teaching."

13. Fred A. Bonner II et al., eds., *Black Faculty in the Academy: Narratives for Negotiating Identity and Achieving Career Success* (Routledge, 2014).

14. Pittman, "Race and Gender Oppression in the Classroom."

15. Vargas, "When the 'Other' Is the Teacher."

16. Moore, "Inappropriate Challenges to Professional Authority," 204.

17. Pittman, "Race and Gender Oppression in the Classroom."

18. C. Turner, J. C. Gonzalez, and J. Wood, "Faculty of Color in Academe: What 20 Years of Literature Tells Us," *Journal of Diversity in Higher Education* 1, no. 3 (2008): 139–68.

19. Vargas, "When the 'Other' Is the Teacher."

20. Taylor, Taylor, and Rode, "Contrapower Harassment in the Sport Management Classroom"; Colleen Flaherty, "Belly of the Beast: Sociologists Call for a Systematic Response to Online Targeting of and Threats against Public Scholars," 2017, https://www.insidehighered.com/news/2017/08/14/sociologists-seek-systematic-response-online-targeting-and-threats-against-public.

21. Saida Grundy, "A History of White Violence Tells Us Attacks on Black Academics Are Not Ending (I Know Because It Happened to Me)," *Ethnic and Racial Studies* 40, no. 11 (September 2017): 1864–71; Abby L. Ferber, "'Are You Willing to Die for This Work?' Public Targeted Online Harassment in Higher Education: SWS Presidential Address," *Gender & Society* 32, no. 3 (June 1, 2018): 301–20, https://doi.org/10.1177/0891243218766831.

22. Robert Boice, "Classroom Incivilities," *Research in Higher Education* 37, no. 4 (1996): 453–86; Robert Boice, *Advice for New Faculty Members: Nihil Nimus* (Allyn & Bacon, 2000); Alan Seidman, "The Learning Killer: Disruptive Student Behavior in the Classroom," *Reading Improvement* 42, no. 1 (Spring 2005): 40–46.

23. Boice, *Advice for New Faculty Members*; Amy Hirschy and John Braxton, "Effects of Student Classroom Incivilities on Students," *New Directions for Teaching and Learning*, 2004, no. 99 (2004): 67–76.

24. R. L. Dukes and G. Victoria, "The Effects of Gender, Status, and Effective Teaching on the Evaluation of College Instruction," *Teaching Sociology* 17 (1989): 447–57; C. J. Fries and R. J. McNinch, "Signed Versus Unsigned Student Evaluations of Teaching: A Comparison," *Teaching Sociology* 31, no. 3 (2003): 333–44; D. S. Hamermesh and A. M.

Parker, "Beauty in the Classroom: Instructors' Pulchritude and Putative Pedagogical Productivity," *Economics of Education Review* 24, no. 4 (2005): 369–76; JoAnn Miller and Marilyn Chamberlin, "Women Are Teachers, Men Are Professors: A Study of Student Perceptions," *Teaching Sociology* 28 (2000): 283–98; J. E. Williams et al., "The Color of Teachers, the Color of Students: The Multicultural Classroom Experience," *Teaching Sociology* 27, no. 3 (1999): 233–51; D. L. Rubin, "Help! My Professor (or Doctor or Boss) Doesn't Talk English." in *Readings in Cultural Contexts*, ed. J. N. Martin, T. K. Nakayama, and L. A. Flores (Mayfield, 2001), 127–40; S. Lazos, "Are Student Teaching Evaluations Holding Back Women and Minorities: The Perils of Doing Gender and Race in the Classroom," in *Presumed Incompetent: The Intersections of Race and Class for Women in Academia*, ed. G. Gutiérrez et al. (Utah State University Press, 2012), 164–85.

25. Boice, *Advice for New Faculty Members*; C. Castro, "In the Margins of the Academy: Women of Color and Job Satisfaction," in *Dilemmas of Black Faculty at U.S. Predominantly White Institutions: Issues in the Post-Multicultural Era*, ed. S. E. Moore and R. Alexander Jr (Edwin Mellen Press, 2010), 136–57; G. Gutiérrez et al., *Presumed Incompetent: The Intersections of Race and Class for Women in Academia* (Utah State University Press, 2012); A. Schneider, "Insubordination and Intimidation Signal the End of Decorum in Many Classrooms," *Chronicle of Higher Education* 44, no. 29 (1998): 12–14; Roxanna Zambrana, *Toxic Ivory Towers: The Health Consequences of Work Stress on the Health of Underrepresented Minority Faculty* (Rutgers University Press, 2018).

26. Walter R. Allen et al., "Outsiders within: Race, Gender, and Faculty Status in U. S. Higher Education," in *The Racial Crisis in American Higher Education: Continuing Challenges for the Twenty-First Century*, ed. W. A. Smith, P. G. Altbach, and K. Lomotey (SUNY University Press, 2002): 189–220; O Villalpando and D Delgado, "A Critical Race Theory Analysis of Barriers That Impede the Success of Faculty of Color," in *The Racial Crisis in American Higher Education: Continuing Challenges for the Twenty-First Century*, ed. W. A. Smith, P. G. Altbach, and K. Lomotey (State University of New York Press, 2002), 243–69.

27. B. A. Berger, "Incivility," *American Journal of Pharmaceutical Education* 64 (2000): 445–50; Cynthia Clark, "The Dance of Incivility in Nursing Education as Described by Nursing Faculty and Students," *Advances in Nursing Science* 31, no. 4 (2008): E37–54; P. J. Morrissette, "Reducing Incivility in the University/College Classroom," *International Electronic Journal for Leadership in Learning* 5 (2001): 1–12.

28. Lisa A. Burke et al., "Student Incivility: A Domain Review," *Journal of Management Education* 38, no. 2 (2014): 14.

29. E.g., Christian A. Meissner and John C. Brigham, "Thirty Years of Investigating the Own-Race Bias in Memory for Faces: A Meta-Analytic Review," *Psychology, Public Policy, and Law* 7, no. 1 (2001): 3–35.

30. Brittany S. Cassidy et al., "Configural Face Processing Impacts Race Disparities in Humanization and Trust," *Journal of Experimental Social Psychology* 73 (2017): 111–24.

31. Pittman, "Race and Gender Oppression in the Classroom."

32. E.g., McGowan, "Multicultural Teaching"; Harlow, "Race Doesn't Matter, but . . ."; Kardia and Wright, "Instructor Identity"; Pittman, "Race and Gender Oppression in the Classroom"; Rubin, "Help! My Professor (or Doctor or Boss) Doesn't Talk English."

33. Pittman, "Race and Gender Oppression in the Classroom."

34. E.g., Pittman, "Race and Gender Oppression in the Classroom"; Kardia and Wright, "Instructor Identity"; Harlow, "Race Doesn't Matter, but . . ."

35. E.g., Pittman, *Incivility in the Classroom*.

Chapter 4

1. American University, "The Benefits of Inclusion and Diversity in the Classroom, July 24, 2019, by School of Education Online Program," School of Education Online Programs, July 24, 2019; Drexel University School of Education, "The Importance of Diversity & Multicultural Awareness in Education," June 23, 2023, https://drexel.edu/soe/resources/student-teaching/advice/importance-of-cultural-diversity-in-classroom/; University of California, "Diversity in the Classroom" (UCLA Diversity & Faculty Development by University of California, 2014).

2. bell hooks, *Teaching to Transgress: Education as the Practice of Freedom* (Routledge, 1994), 37.

3. E.g., Kimberly A. Griffin, "Looking Beyond the Pipeline: Institutional Barriers, Strategies, and Benefits to Increasing the Representation of Women and Men of Color in the Professoriate," in *Higher Education: Handbook of Theory and Research*, ed. Laura W. Perna, 35 (Springer International, 2020): 1–73.

4. James Bohman, "Critical Theory," in *Stanford Encyclopedia of Philosophy* (Spring 2021 Edition), ed. Edward N. Zalta, 2021, https://plato.stanford.edu/archives/spr2021/entries/critical-theory.

5. E.g., Ginny Jones Boss et al., "'It's a Double-Edged Sword': A Collaborative Autoethnography of Women of Color Higher Education and Student Affairs Administrators Who Teach in the College Classroom," *Journal of Women and Gender in Higher Education* 12, no. 2 (2019): 166–85; Griffin, "Looking Beyond the Pipeline"; bell hooks, *Teaching to Transgress: Education as the Practice of Freedom* (Routledge, 1994); Dalia Rodriguez et al., "Practicing Liberatory Pedagogy: Women of Color in College Classrooms," *Cultural Studies ↔ Critical Methodologies* 12, no. 2 (2012): 96–108; Leonard Taylor and Cameron C. Beatty, "Toward a Liberatory Praxis for Emerging Black Faculty," in *In Diversity, Equity, and Inclusivity in Contemporary Higher Education*, ed. Rhonda Jeffries, IGI Global (2019), 108–21.

6. hooks, *Teaching to Transgress*.

7. Pablo Freire, *Pedagogy of the Oppressed* (Seabury Press, 1970).

8. bell hooks, *Teaching Critical Thinking: Practical Wisdom* (Routledge, 2010), 9–10.

9. Christopher P. Dwyer, Michael J. Hogan, and Ian Stewart, "An Integrated Critical Thinking Framework for the 21st Century," *Thinking Skills & Creativity* 12 (2014): 43–52; Christopher P. Dwyer, *Critical Thinking: Conceptual Perspectives and Practical Guidelines* (Cambridge University Press, 2017).

10. Karl Marx, Friedrich Engels, and Robert C. Tucker, *The Marx-Engels Reader* (W. W. Norton & Company, 1978).

11. Quintin Hoare and Geoffrey Nowell-Smith, eds., *Selections from the Prison Notebooks of Antonio Gramsci* (Lawrence & Wishart, 1971).

12. Joseph V. Femia, *Gramsci's Political Thought: Hegemony, Consciousness, and the Revolutionary Process* (Clarendon Press, 1981).

13. Patricia Hill Collins, *Black Feminist Thought: Knowledge, Consciousness, and the Politics of Empowerment* (Routledge, 2002).

14. Anthony Lising Antonio, "Faculty of Color Reconsidered: Reassessing Contributions to Scholarship," *Journal of Higher Education* 73, no. 5 (2002): 582–602; C. Turner, J. C. Gonzalez, and J. Wood, "Faculty of Color in Academe: What 20 Years of Literature Tells Us," *Journal of Diversity in Higher Education* 1, no. 3 (2008): 139–68; Ellen Bara Stolzenberg et al., "Undergraduate Teaching Faculty: The HERI Faculty Survey 2016–2017" (Higher Education Research Institute: UCLA, 2019); Griffin, "Looking Beyond the Pipeline"; Rodriguez et al., "Practicing Liberatory Pedagogy"; Jones Boss et al., "'It's a Double-Edged Sword'"; Taylor and Beatty, "Toward a Liberatory Praxis for Emerging Black Faculty"; Christen Priddie et al., "Centering Black Women Faculty: Magnifying Powerful

Voices," *To Improve the Academy: A Journal of Educational Development* 41, no. 2 (2022): 96–127.

15. Florida State University, "Mission and Vision," accessed April 4, 2025, https://www.fsu.edu/about/mission-vision.html.

16. University of Iowa, "About Iowa," accessed April 4, 2025, https://uiowa.edu/about-iowa.

17. Bowdoin, "The Mission of the College," accessed April 4, 2025, https://www.bowdoin.edu/about/mission/index.html.

18. Massachusetts Institute of Technology, "About MIT," accessed April 2, 2025, https://web.mit.edu/about/.

19. University of California Los Angeles, "Our Vision, Mission and Principles," accessed April 2, 2025, https://www.ucla.edu/about/mission-and-values.

20. A note for teaching in contexts that are anti-DEI or anti-academic freedom: Almost all accrediting bodies currently have some sort of diversity, cultural, global, intellectual growth, societal contribution, etc. requirement for student learning. As mentioned previously, nothing will make you untouchable. That said, this accreditation requirement and relevant non-DEI university goals will provide leverage as you, allies, colleagues, institutions, and organizations safeguard your career.

21. E.g., Sylvia Hurtado, Sylvia Ruiz Alvarado, and Chelsea Guillermo-Wann, "Creating Inclusive Environments: The Mediating Effect of Faculty and Staff Validation on the Relationship of Discrimination/Bias to Students' Sense of Belonging," *Journal Committed to Social Change on Race and Ethnicity* 1, no. 1 (2015): 60–81; Michael W. Asher et al., "Utility-Value Intervention Promotes Persistence and Diversity in STEM," *Proceedings of the National Academy of Sciences*, 120, no. 19 (2023), article id.e2300463120, https://www.pnas.org/doi/10.1073/pnas.2300463120; Amanda LaTasha Armstrong, "The Representation of Social Groups in U. S. Educational Materials and Why It Matters: A Research Overview," December 1, 2021, https://www.newamerica.org/education-policy/reports/the-representation-of-social-groups-in-u-s-educational-materials-and-why-it-matter/.

Chapter 5

1. Bonnie Tusmith and Maureen T. Reddy, eds., *Race in the College Classroom: Pedagogy and Politics* (Rutgers University Press, 2002); Chavella T. Pittman, "Race and Gender Oppression in the Classroom: The Experiences of Women Faculty of Color with White Male Students,"

Teaching Sociology 38, no. 3 (July 1, 2010): 183–96; American Sociological Association, "Statement on Student Evaluations of Teaching," 2019, https://www.asanet.org/wp-content/uploads/asa_statement_on_student_evaluations_of_teaching_feb132020.pdf).

2. Maryellen Weimer, *Learner-Centered Teaching: Five Key Changes to Practice*, 2nd ed. (Jossey-Bass, 2013); Linda B. Nilson, *Teaching at Its Best: A Research-Based Resource for College Instructor* (John Wiley & Sons, 2016).

3. Ellen Bara Stolzenberg et al., "Undergraduate Teaching Faculty: The HERI Faculty Survey 2016–2017" (Higher Education Research Institute: UCLA, 2019); Maryellen Weimer, "Instructional Techniques: Those Used and Those Perceived to Promote Learning," *The Teaching Professor* 27, no.3 (Magna Publications, 2013): 7; William J. Lammers and John J. Murphy, "A Profile of Teaching Techniques Used in the University Classroom: A Descriptive Profile of a US Public University," *Active Learning in Higher Education* 3, no. 1 (2002): 54–67.

4. Anthony Lising Antonio, "Faculty of Color Reconsidered: Reassessing Contributions to Scholarship," *Journal of Higher Education* 73, no. 5 (2002): 582–602; Anita Casavantes Bradford and Alberto Eduardo Morales, "Toward a Critical Latinx Pedagogy: A Multi-Generational Reflection on Teaching and Learning in the U.S. Latinx History Survey and Beyond," *Journal of Latinos and Education* 22, no. 3 (2023): 1107–17; Stolzenberg et al., "Undergraduate Teaching Faculty: The HERI Faculty Survey 2016–2017"; Shirley Hune, "Chapter 14 Asian American Women Faculty and the Contested Space of the Classroom: Navigating Student Resistance and (Re)Claiming Authority and Their Rightful Place," in *Women of Color in Higher Education: Turbulent Past, Promising Future (Diversity in Higher Education*, ed. Jean-Marie Gaetane and Brenda Lloyd-Jones, Vol. 9 (Emerald Group, 2011), 307–35; C. Turner, J. C. Gonzalez, and J. Wood, "Faculty of Color in Academe: What 20 Years of Literature Tells Us," *Journal of Diversity in Higher Education* 1, no. 3 (2008): 139–68; Kimberly A. Griffin, "Looking Beyond the Pipeline: Institutional Barriers, Strategies, and Benefits to Increasing the Representation of Women and Men of Color in the Professoriate," in *Higher Education: Handbook of Theory and Research*, ed. Laura W. Perna, 35 (Springer International, 2020): 1–73.

5. Antonio, "Faculty of Color Reconsidered."

6. M. F. Knowles and B. W. Harleston, *Achieving Diversity in the Professorate: Challenges and Opportunities* (American Council on Education, 1997).

7. Antonio, "Faculty of Color Reconsidered"; P. D. Umbach, "The Contribution of Faculty of Color to Undergraduate Education," *Research in Higher Education* 47, no. 3 (2006): 317–45; Stolzenberg et al., "Undergraduate Teaching Faculty: The HERI Faculty Survey 2016–2017"; Sylvia Hurtado et al., "Undergraduate Teaching Faculty: The 2010–2011 HERI Faculty Survey" (Higher Education Research Institute, UCLA, 2012).

8. Hune, "Chapter 14 Asian American Women Faculty and the Contested Space of the Classroom"; Casavantes Bradford and Morales, "Toward a Critical Latinx Pedagogy"; Umbach, "The Contribution of Faculty of Color to Undergraduate Education."

9. O Villalpando and D Delgado, "A Critical Race Theory Analysis of Barriers That Impede the Success of Faculty of Color," in *The Racial Crisis in American Higher Education: Continuing Challenges for the Twenty-First Century*, ed. W. A. Smith, P. G. Altbach, and K. Lomotey (State University of New York Press, 2002), 243–69; Kimberly A. Griffin, "Looking Beyond the Pipeline: Institutional Barriers, Strategies, and Benefits to Increasing the Representation of Women and Men of Color in the Professoriate," in *Higher Education: Handbook of Theory and Research*, ed. Laura W. Perna, 35 (Springer International, 2020): 1–73; Walter R. Allen et al., "Outsiders within: Race, Gender, and Faculty Status in U. S. Higher Education," in *The Racial Crisis in American Higher Education: Continuing Challenges for the Twenty-First Century*, ed. W. A. Smith, P. G. Altbach, and K. Lomotey (SUNY University Press, 2002): 189–220.

10. Pittman, "Race and Gender Oppression in the Classroom"; Saida Grundy, "A History of White Violence Tells Us Attacks on Black Academics Are Not Ending (I Know Because It Happened to Me)," *Ethnic and Racial Studies* 40, no. 11 (September 2017): 1864–71; Hune, "Chapter 14 Asian American Women Faculty and the Contested Space of the Classroom"; Griffin, "Looking Beyond the Pipeline"; American Sociological Association, "Statement on Student Evaluations of Teaching."

11. Chavella T. Pittman, "The Overlooked Minefield," *Inside Higher Ed*, April 15, 2021.

12. Christine A. Stanley and Erin M. Porte, eds., *Engaging Large Classes: Strategies and Techniques for College Faculty* (Anker Publishing Company, 2002); Nilson, *Teaching at Its Best*; Tracie Marcella Addy et al., *What Inclusive Instructors Do: Principles and Practices for Excellence in College Teaching* (Stylus, 2021); Joshua R. Eyler, *How Humans Learn: The*

Science and Stories behind Effective College Teaching (West Virginia University Press, 2018); Michelle D. Miller, *Minds Online: Teaching Effectively with Technology* (Harvard University Press, 2014); Kevin Kelly and Todd Zakrajsek, *Advancing Online Teaching: Creating Equity-Based Digital Learning Environments* (Routledge, 2021); Thomas J. Tobin and Kirsten T. Behling, *Reach Everyone, Teach Everyone: Universal Design for Learning in Higher Education* (West Virginia University Press, 2018); Michelle D. Miller, *Remembering and Forgetting in the Age of Technology: Teaching, Learning, and the Science of Memory in a Wired World* (West Virginia University Press, 2022).

13. Michelle D. Miller, Conducted by Chavella T. Pittman, March 23, 2022; Joshua R. Eyler, Conducted by Chavella T. Pittman, March 24, 2022; Thomas Tobin, Conducted by Chavella T. Pittman, March 25, 2022.

14. Miller, *Remembering and Forgetting in the Age of Technology*.

15. Miller, *Minds Online*.

16. Miller, Conducted by Chavella T. Pittman.

17. Miller, Conducted by Chavella T. Pittman.

18. Eyler, *How Humans Learn*.

19. Eyler, Conducted by Chavella T. Pittman.

20. Tobin and Behling, *Reach Everyone, Teach Everyone*.

21. Tobin, Conducted by Chavella T. Pittman.

22. Charles C. Bonwell and James A. Eisen, "Active Learning: Creating Excitement in the Classroom" (School of Education and Human Development: George Washington University: 1991); S. Freeman et al., "Active Learning Increases Student Performance in Science, Engineering, and Mathematics," *Proceedings of the National Academy of Sciences* 111, no. 23 (2014): 8410–15, https://doi.org/10.1073/pnas.1319030111; M. Prince, "Does Active Learning Work? A Review of the Research," *Journal of Engineering Education* 93, no. 3 (2004): 223–31, https://doi.org/10.1002/j.2168-9830.2004.tb00809.x; Richard R. Hake, "Interactive-Engagement versus Traditional Methods: A Six-Thousand-Student Survey of Mechanics Test Data for Introductory Physics Courses," *American Journal of Physics* 66, no. 1 (1998): 64–74.

23. Massachusetts Institute of Technology, "About MIT," accessed June 26, 2023, https://web.mit.edu/about/.

24. Carol Ann Tomlinson et al., "Differentiating Instruction in Response to Student Readiness, Interest, and Learning Profile in Academically Diverse Classrooms: A Review of Literature," *Journal for the Education of the Gifted* 27, no. 2/3 (2003): 119–45.

25. American Psychological Association, "Learner-Centered Psychological Principles: Guidelines for School Redesign and Reform" (Washington, DC, 1992).

26. Arthur Chickering and Zelda Gamson, "'Seven Principles for Good Practice in Undergraduate Education,'" *AAHE Bulletin* 39, no. 7 (1987): 6.

27. Barbara Gross Davis, *Tools for Teaching* (Jossey-Bass, 1993): 192.

28. Jill Whalen, "More Is More: Multiple Measures for Better Assessment," July 1, 2016, https://www.anthology.com/blog/more-is-more-multiple-measures-for-better-assessment.

29. Miller: *Remembering and Forgetting in the Age of Technology*.

30. Chickering and Gamson, "Seven Principles for Good Practice in Undergraduate Education".

31. Barbara Gross Davis, *Tools for Teaching* (Jossey-Bass, 1993): 192.

Chapter 6

1. Allison Daminger, "The Cognitive Dimension of Household Labor," *American Sociological Review* 84, no. 4 (2019): 609–33.

2. Roxanna Harlow, "Race Doesn't Matter, but . . . : The Effect of Race on Professors' Experiences and Emotion Management in the Undergraduate College Classroom," *Social Psychology Quarterly* 66, no. 4 (2003): 348–63; Ersula Ore, "Pushback: A Pedagogy of Care," *Pedagogy* 17, no. 1 (January 2017): 9–33; Sarah Rose Cavanagh and Joshua R. Eyler, "Building a Pedagogy of Care with Social and Emotional Presence," ed. Victoria Mondelli and Thomas J. Tobin, 2020, https://www.youtube.com/watch?v=11FUuLBVOAc&feature=youtu.be; Amani El-Alayli, Ashley Hansen-Brown, and Michelle Ceynar, "Dancing Backwards in High Heels: Female Professors Experience More Work Demands and Special Favor Requests," *Particularly from Academically Entitled Students. Sex Roles* 79, no. 3–4 (2018): 136–50.

3. Joya Misra et al., "Gendered and Racialized Perceptions of Faculty Workloads," *Gender & Society* 35, no. 3 (2021): 358–94; Catherine White Berheide, Megan A. Carpenter, and David A. Cotter, "Teaching College in the Time of COVID-19," *Gender and Race Differences in Faculty Emotional Labor. Sex Roles* 86 (2022): 441–55.

4. Kimberly A. Griffin, "Looking Beyond the Pipeline: Institutional Barriers, Strategies, and Benefits to Increasing the Representation of Women and Men of Color in the Professoriate," in *Higher*

Education: Handbook of Theory and Research, ed. Laura W. Perna, 35 (Springer International, 2020): 1–73; C. Pittman, "Race & Gender Oppression in the Classroom: The Experiences of Women Faculty of Color with White Male Students," *Teaching Sociology* 38, no. 3 (2010): 183–96; Claudia Lampman, "Women Faculty at Risk: U.S. Professors Report on Their Experiences with Student Incivility, Bullying, Aggression, and Sexual Attention," *NASPA Journal About Women in Higher Education* 5, no. 2 (2012): 184–208.

5. El-Alayli, Hansen-Brown, and Ceynar, "Dancing Backwards in High Heels"; Pittman, "Race & Gender Oppression in the Classroom"; Berheide, Carpenter, and Cotter, "Teaching College in the Time of COVID-19."

6. Elizabeth Torres Carpio, "Street-Level Educators: The Selective Recognition of Students and Invisible TA Labor," *Work and Occupations* 51, no. 1 (2024): 25–46; Berheide, Carpenter, and Cotter, "Teaching College in the Time of COVID-19."

7. Roxanne Harlow, "Race Doesn't Matter, but . . ."; Ryan A. Miller, Cathy D. Howell, and Laura Struve, "'Constantly, Excessively, and All the Time': The Emotional Labor of Teaching Diversity Courses," *International Journal of Teaching and Learning in Higher Education* 31, no. 3 (2019): 491–502; Torres Carpio, "Street-Level Educators."

8. Marcia L. Bellas, "Emotional Labor in Academia: The Case of Professors," *The Annals of the American Academy of Political and Social Science* 561 (1999): 96–110; Sekile M. Nzinga-Johnson, ed., *Laboring Positions: Black Women, Mothering and the Academy* (Demeter Press, 2013); Misra et al., "Gendered and Racialized Perceptions of Faculty Workloads."

9. C. Castro, "In the Margins of the Academy: Women of Color and Job Satisfaction," in *Dilemmas of Black Faculty at U.S. Predominantly White Institutions: Issues in the Post-Multicultural Era*, ed. S. E. Moore and R. Alexander Jr (Edwin Mellen Press, 2010), 136–57; Zaynab Sabagh, Nathan C. Hall, and Alenoush Saroya, "Antecedents, Correlates and Consequences of Faculty Burnout," *Educational Research* 60, no. 2 (2018): 131–56; Ruth. E. Zambrana et al., "Workplace Stress and Discrimination Effects on the Physical and Depressive Symptoms of Underrepresented Minority Faculty," *Stress and Health: Journal of the International Society for the Investigation of Stress* 37, no. 1 (2021): 175–85, https://doi.org/10.1002/smi.2983.

10. Daniel J. Madigan and Lisa E. Kim, "Does Teacher Burnout Affect Students? A Systematic Review of Its Association with Academic

Achievement and Student-Reported Outcomes," *International Journal of Educational Research* 105 (2021), https://www.sciencedirect.com/science/article/abs/pii/S0883035520318206; Sabagh, Hall, and Saroya, "Antecedents, Correlates and Consequences of Faculty Burnout."

11. El-Alayli, Hansen-Brown, and Ceynar, "Dancing Backwards in High Heels"; Berheide, Carpenter, and Cotter, "Teaching College in the Time of COVID-19"; Pittman, "Race & Gender Oppression in the Classroom"; Constance M. Ruzich, "Are You My Mother? Students' Expectations of Teachers and Teaching as Related to Faculty Gender" (Annual Meeting of the Conference on College Composition and Communication, 46th Washington DC, 1995), 24.

12. Jessie Shirley Bernard, *Academic Women* (Penn State University Press, 1964); Nzinga-Johnson, *Laboring Positions*; Sekile M. Nzinga-Johnson, *Lean Semesters: How Higher Education Reproduces Inequity*, Critical University Studies (Johns Hopkins University Press, 2020).

13. Robert Boice, *Advice for New Faculty Members: Nihil Nimus* (Allyn & Bacon, 2000); Nicki Monahan, MEd, "More Content Doesn't Equal More Learning," October 12, 2015, https://www.facultyfocus.com/articles/effective-teaching-strategies/more-content-doesnt-equal-more-learning/.

14. Boice, *Advice for New Faculty Members*; Christina I. Petersen et al., "The Tyranny of Content: 'Content Coverage' as a Barrier to Evidence-Based Teaching Approaches and Ways to Overcome It," *CBE Life Sci Educ.* 19, no. 2 (June 2020): ar17.

15. Jeffrey Schinske and Kimberly Tanner, "Teaching More by Grading Less (or Differently)," *CBE Life Sciences Education* 13, no. 2 (2014): 159–66; John Sweller and Paul Chandler, "Evidence for Cognitive Load Theory," *Cognition and Instruction* 8, no. 4 (1991): 351–62.

16. Joshua R. Eyler, "Grades Are at the Center of the Student Mental Health Crisis," *Inside Higher Education*, March 7, 2022, https://www.insidehighered.com/blogs/just-visiting/grades-are-center-student-mental-health-crisis; Linda Burzotta Nilson, *Specifications Grading: Restoring Rigor, Motivating Students, and Saving Faculty Time* (Stylus, 2015); Boice, *Advice for New Faculty Members*; Barbara E. Walvoord and Virginia Johnson Anderson, *Effective Grading: A Tool for Learning and Assessment*, 2nd ed. (Jossey-Bass, 2009).

17. Kerry Ann Rockquemore, "The Teaching Trap," March 14, 2010, https://www.insidehighered.com/advice/2010/03/15/teaching-trap.

18. James M. Lang, *Small Teaching: Everyday Lessons From the Science of Learning* (Jossey-Bass, 2021); Flower Darby and James M. Lang, *Small*

Teaching Online: Applying Learning Science in Online Classes (John Wiley & Sons, 2019); Linda B. Nilson, *Teaching at Its Best: A Research-Based Resource for College Instructors*, 3rd ed. (Jossey-Bass, 2010).

19. Harlow, "Race Doesn't Matter, but..."; El-Alayli, Hansen-Brown, and Ceynar, "Dancing Backwards in High Heels"; Nzinga-Johnson, *Laboring Positions*.

20. Cavanagh and Eyler, "Building a Pedagogy of Care with Social and Emotional Presence"; Jessamyn Neuhaus, "Pedagogy Nerds Assemble! Battling Big Myths about Teaching in Troubled Times," ed. Victoria Mondelli and Thomas J. Tobin, Pedagogies of Care: Open Resources for Student-Centered & Adaptive Strategies in the New Higher-Ed Landscap, 2020, https://sabresmonkey.wixsite.com/pedagogiesofcare; Carleton University Science Education Resource Center, "Immediacy in the Classroom: Research and Practical Implications," https://serc.carleton.edu/NAGTWorkshops/affective/immediacy.html.

21. John Sweller, "Cognitive Load During Problem Solving," *Cognitive Science* 12 (1988): 257–85; Sweller and Chandler, "Evidence for Cognitive Load Theory."

22. Walvoord and Johnson Anderson, *Effective Grading*; Rockquemore, "The Teaching Trap"; Misra et al., "Gendered and Racialized Perceptions of Faculty Workloads"; Jayne R. Goode, "Instruction on the Front Lines: Student Trauma and Secondary Traumatic Stress among University Faculty," *Communication Education* 72, no. 2 (December 2022): 1–19; Sabagh, Hall, and Saroya, "Antecedents, Correlates and Consequences of Faculty Burnout."

23. Carleton University Science Education Resource Center, "Immediacy in the Classroom"; Sheridan Library and Learning Center, "Online Teaching and Learning: Creating the Conditions for (Online) Learning," accessed June 21, 2023, https://sheridancollege.libguides.com/c.php?g=715931&p=5105241; Vanderbilt Center for Teaching, "International Instructor Guide," n.d., https://cft.vanderbilt.edu/guides-sub-pages/international-instructor-guide/, accessed June 21, 2023; Neuhaus, "Pedagogy Nerds Assemble! Battling Big Myths about Teaching in Troubled Times."

24. Nzinga-Johnson, *Laboring Positions*; Misra et al., "Gendered and Racialized Perceptions of Faculty Workloads."

25. Torres Carpio, "Street-Level Educators"; Nzinga-Johnson, *Lean Semesters*; Zambrana et al., "Workplace Stress and Discrimination Effects on the Physical and Depressive Symptoms of Underrepresented

Minority Faculty"; Miller, Howell, and Struve, "'Constantly, Excessively, and All the Time'"; Madeline Will, "Teachers Are Not OK, Even Though We Need Them to Be," *Education Week*, September 14, 2021, https://www.edweek.org/teaching-learning/teachers-are-not-ok-even-though-we-need-them-to-be/2021/09#:~:text=Research%20shows%20that%20when%20teachers,their%20academic%20performance%20and%20engagement.

26. Edward Hebert, "Faculty Morale: A Perspective for Academic Leaders," *Kinesiology Review* 8, no. 4 (2019): 305–11; Sabagh, Hall, and Saroya, "Antecedents, Correlates and Consequences of Faculty Burnout."

Appendix

1. Frances E. Kendall, Ph.D., "How to Be an Ally If You Are a Person with Privilege," 2003, http://www.scn.org/friends/ally.html.

2. Chavella Pittman, "Colleges Must Change to Retain BIPOC Women Faculty," *Inside Higher Ed*, April 30, 2021, https://www.insidehighered.com/advice/2021/04/30/retain-bipoc-women-faculty-colleges-must-remove-obstacles-they-face-opinion.

3. Pittman, "Colleges Must Change to Retain BIPOC Women Faculty."

4. Pittman, "Colleges Must Change to Retain BIPOC Women Faculty."

INDEX

academic freedom, 2, 31–34, 36–37, 106
administrators, 8, 18, 21, 140, 147, 151, 165, 167, 169, 173. *See also* deans; department chairs; provosts
advising, 15, 40, 117, 130, 145, 151, 172
affective labor, 140–42, 144–49, 151, 156, 162
anchor points, 43–59
appearance, physical, 137, 143
approachability, 77, 146
authenticity, 4, 8, 16, 22, 34, 111, 144; and teaching innovation, 114, 120, 122, 124, 126, 130–32
authority, 5, 18, 20, 33–35, 65, 72, 78–82, 136, 142, 168

Beast, the, 136–37; energy required for, 138–44; consequences of 144–45
behavior management, 64–71, 73, 75–84. *See also* Classroom Behavior Expectations Statements
biology of learning, 120, 122–23, 127–29, 132
burnout, 20, 37, 61, 74, 144, 157. *See also* energy

campuses, 2–3, 7, 13–18, 73, 78, 112, 136, 143, 161; equitable, 21, 41, 45, 80, 83, 104–7, 109, 165. *See also* mission statements, institutional
careers, 1–3, 17, 31, 62; and classroom management, 73–75, 79, 82; and diverse and multiple perspectives, 87, 90, 96, 104; and invisible labor, 39, 42, 52, 60–61, 84, 140, 144–45; and joy, 134–36, 146–49, 152, 162; protection of, 9, 22–24, 35–36, 120; and resistance to WFOC, 17, 19–21; and teaching, 10, 114, 118–19, 124, 130–31, 157; and time, 155–57, 162. *See also* threats; threats, career
caring labor, 142, 146, 151–56
chairs. *See* department chairs
Classroom Behavior Expectations Statements, 67, 71, 73, 80, 170
classrooms, 4, 13, 37, 171; and diverse and multiple perspectives, 15, 89–90, 92, 96–98, 100, 103, 108; and invisible labor, 39–45, 58–59, 138–41, 143; and joy, 147, 158–63; and management, 62–84, 150, 170; and resistance to WFOC, 17, 19–21, 32–35, 111; and teaching practices, 52, 54–56, 60, 86–88, 112–15, 117–18, 121–23, 131; and time, 155–57. *See also* Classroom Behavior Expectations Statements; disruptions, classroom; incivilities; teaching
cognitive dissonance, 97, 99, 101
cognitive labor, 138–40, 144–49, 151, 156, 162
colleagues, 3, 5–6; and ally actions, 165–67, 169, 173; and classroom management, 62, 64, 72–75, 81; and diverse and multiple perspectives, 54–55, 91–101, 103–4, 107–9; and invisible labor, 43, 48, 59–60, 139–40, 141–43, 146–47; and joy, 159, 162; and learning

209

outcomes, 53–56; and privilege, 33–35, 57, 78, 80; and resistance to WFOC, 13, 17, 19, 23, 136–37; and reviews, 7, 20–21, 127; and teaching, 14, 28, 30, 111–14, 117–21, 127, 131–35, 147; and time, 151, 153.

committees, 39–40, 171

courses, 15–16, 36, 140; and classroom management, 65–67, 74, 78; and course goals, 23, 25, 28–33, 51–52, 54, 89, 95; and course material, 141, 147–48, 154; and course preparation, 7, 30–31, 63, 117, 138, 149; and course topics, 85–86, 109, 125, 152; and diverse and multiple perspectives, 91–94, 96, 100–104, 106–10, 170; and enrollment levels, 5, 143, 172; and grading, 7, 63, 72, 113, 137–38, 145, 148, 150; and innovation, 126–27, 129; and joy, 135, 147, 158–60; and knowledge, 24, 26, 45–48; and readings, 30, 63, 72, 117, 126–27, 129, 137, 153; and resistance to WFOC, 5, 18, 20, 137, 143; and service courses, 5, 172; and time, 149–50, 152–53, 163. *See also* classrooms; reviews, teaching; syllabi

credit, 35, 59, 104, 109. *See also* tenure credit/currency

deans, 18, 63, 73, 103

demand, use, and discard phenomenon (DUD), 39

department chairs, 18, 73, 130, 142–43

discrimination, 66, 73, 136, 139. *See also* intolerance; oppression; racism; sexism

disruptions, classroom, 66–67, 70–73, 75, 78, 83, 142–43, 145. *See also* incivilities

diverse and multiple perspectives, 7, 44, 87–96, 98–110, 170

emotional labor, 21, 138, 142–49, 151, 156, 162

emotional well-being, 2, 9, 52, 73, 81–82, 144, 154, 158, 160, 179

#empoweredWFOC, 60, 83, 132

empowering actions, 10; and classroom management, 83–84; and diverse and multiple perspectives, 109–10; and invisible teaching labor, 60–61; and teaching futures, 162–63; and teaching innovation, 132–33; and teaching statements, 36–37. *See also* empowerment

empowerment, 1–2, 4, 8–10, 156; and classrooms, 62–64, 66, 70–71, 75, 79–82, 84; and diverse and multiple perspectives, 94, 102, 104, 109–10, 124; and invisible labor, 42, 59; and joy, 135, 146; and resistance to WFOC, 17, 19–23; and students, 15, 25; and teaching, 29, 31, 33, 35–37, 86, 114, 132, 135, 144. *See also* empowering actions

energy, 10, 18–19, 63–64, 72, 81, 96, 163, 172; and invisible labor, 138–39, 145; and teaching, 22, 24, 61, 84, 133–34, 148–56, 158–61. *See also* burnout

exhaustion, 139–40, 144, 157, 161–62

expertise, 4, 34–35, 57, 72, 92–93, 124–25, 127, 131, 172

families, 18, 84, 145, 154–55

flourishing, 65, 71. *See also* thriving

Force Field, 32–33; Empowered Force Field, 34–35

futures, 2, 19–20, 135, 144; and teaching, 147–49, 155–56, 158–63

gender, 4–5, 17, 19, 44, 113, 117, 170; and invisible labor, 138, 140–43, 146–47; and resistance to WFOC, 20, 130, 136–37, 150, 156; and SoTL, 76–79.

grants, 19, 38, 42, 84, 139, 145, 154, 172

INDEX 211

harassment, 18, 66, 73, 79, 83, 143
hostility, 19, 21, 56, 66, 72, 78, 82, 136, 141–43, 160–62
humor, 3, 8, 10, 147

immediacy, pedagogical, 76–77, 151, 154
incivilities, 66, 68, 72–79, 81, 83–84, 150. *See also* disruptions, classroom
innovation, 2, 14–16, 35, 44, 49, 99, 103; and pushback, 126–31; and teaching, 103, 112–26, 132–33, 135, 147
insecurity, 23, 78
institutions, contributions to, 35, 39, 41–42, 102, 104, 109–10, 114, 168
intellectual ideas, 2, 7, 22–23, 86, 89–90, 95, 97–98, 100–101, 105–7
intentionality, 8, 17, 23–24, 29–31, 87, 115, 150, 152, 156–58, 161
invisible labor, 39, 45–50, 52, 61, 138–45. *See also* caring labor; super-invisible labor

joy, 1, 4, 7–8, 31, 66, 79, 120, 165; and invisible labor, 131, 133–36, 138–39, 144; and teaching futures, 147–50, 155–63

Keystone Teaching Statements, 22–32, 35–37
knowledge, 24–27, 29, 90, 149, 166; and diverse and multiple perspectives, 43–51, 58, 86, 88, 93, 95, 97–99, 106–7; and knowledge transfer, 120–22, 126; and norms, 54–56

learning, student, 3, 7, 158, 166; and active learning, 14–16, 29, 68–69, 88, 90, 95, 100, 117, 124; and applied learning, 51–52, 54–55; and biology of learning, 120, 122–23, 127–29, 132; and classroom management, 64–73, 75–76, 80–82; and diverse and multiple perspectives, 87–90, 92–94, 102–4, 110; and experiential learning, 116, 127; and integrative learning, 54–55; and invisible labor, 140–41, 143, 148; and lifelong learning, 49, 51, 105, 107; and outcomes, 35–36, 44–54, 56–60, 95, 160; and passive learning, 69, 88–89, 119, 121; and teaching innovation, 112, 114–15, 117–18, 120–32; and teaching statements, 25–27, 29–30, 32–35; and time, 150–53, 156–57, 160, 163. *See also* Scholarship of Teaching and Learning (SoTL); SoTL Minefields
legitimacy, 35, 56, 91, 96, 101, 108, 136, 141, 162; and illegitimacy, 18–19, 27, 58, 93, 103
loved ones, 7, 139, 154, 161. *See also* families

mainstream perspectives, 40, 47, 52–54, 56, 89–93, 95–97, 99–103, 109; and teaching innovation, 115, 118, 130, 133. *See also* worldviews
marginalization, 18–19, 74, 88, 97, 99–100, 102, 144
mental well-being, 2, 19–20, 74–75, 105, 145, 149, 154, 161
mentoring, 6, 10, 15, 40, 143, 145, 151, 165, 171
mission statements, institutional, 16–17, 104–9, 114, 130
more support for WFOC: ally actions, 169–72; further resources, 179–82; work with Chavella, 37, 60, 84, 110, 133, 163
myths, teaching, 134, 146, 149, 151, 157–58, 162. *See also* stereotypes

neuroscience of learning, 124

open-mindedness, 10, 89, 95, 97
oppression, 15, 118, 130, 136, 138, 150, 162–63; structural, 4, 49, 79, 148, 165

organization of book, 9–11
overperforming, 44, 138–39

pedagogy, 20, 64, 70, 73, 92, 96, 110, 118–19, 130, 169; and care, 146, 151–52, 154–55; innovative and transformative, 14–16, 35, 115–16. *See also* immediacy, pedagogical; teaching
physical well-being, 2, 20, 74–75, 78, 145, 161
power, 13, 32–36, 52–53, 80, 83, 130, 143, 168–69, 173; and diverse and multiple perspectives, 95–96, 99–103, 105, 108
privilege, 67, 78–80, 83, 100, 125; and invisible labor, 143, 146–47; and SoTL, 33–34, 52. *See also* colleagues
productivity, 19, 44, 81–82, 144, 148
promotion, 2, 5, 7–9, 13, 17, 147, 163; and classroom management, 73–74, 84; and diverse and multiple perspectives, 101, 109–10; and invisible labor, 39–43, 45, 50–51, 59–60, 139; and resistance to WFOC, 19–20, 22; and teaching, 29, 36–37, 56, 112–13, 119–20, 130–33, 135; and time, 151, 154. *See also* tenure
protection, 1–2, 8–9, 21–23, 120, 147; and classroom management, 66–67, 70, 75, 79, 81–84, 96; and teaching, 4, 24, 27, 29–37, 57, 61, 130–31, 143
provosts, 103, 130
publications, 19, 42, 84, 103, 141, 145, 154. *See also* scholarship
punishment, 7, 19–20, 147; and diverse and multiple perspectives, 87, 99–101, 103–4, 170; and teaching, 53–54, 63, 77, 112–14, 117–18, 132

race, 4–5, 17–20, 44; and diverse and multiple perspectives, 86, 88–89, 91, 94–96, 99, 101, 137; and invisible labor, 138, 140, 146–47; and resistance to WFOC, 136–38, 141–42, 150, 156; and SoTL, 76–79; and teaching innovation, 113, 117
racism, 18–19, 55, 63, 73, 92, 101, 133, 140–42, 147, 149; and resistance to WFOC, 20–21, 130, 137, 139, 150. *See also* intolerance
renewal, job, 2, 7, 17, 19, 36, 119, 131, 133, 139
research, 7, 53, 169; on classroom management, 66, 72, 74, 76–78; and diverse and multiple perspectives, 91, 93–95, 98, 101, 103, 105–6; on resistance to WFOC, 17, 20; on teaching innovation, 114, 117, 126–27, 129–31; and teaching time, 154–55; used in teaching, 49, 63, 91; on WFOC, 10, 13, 15–16; on WFOC teaching, 36, 44, 47. *See also* evidence-based strategies; scholarship, WFOC; Scholarship of Teaching and Learning (SoTL); SoTL Minefields
resistance to WFOC, 5, 16–23, 30–31, 57, 59–60, 162; and diverse and multiple perspectives, 78, 93–94, 96, 99–104, 108; and invisible labor, 138–39; and teaching innovation, 111, 113–14, 117–20, 126–33
retention, 5, 7–9, 13, 20, 22, 147, 163; and classroom management, 73–74, 84; and diverse and multiple perspectives, 101, 107, 109–10; and super-invisible labor, 41–42, 45, 50, 56, 59–60, 139; and teaching, 29, 37, 56, 112–13, 119–20, 130, 132, 135, 139; and time, 151, 154
reviews, institutional, 4, 6–10, 19, 23; and classroom management, 73–76, 81–84; and diverse and multiple perspectives, 54–56, 94–96, 98–99, 101–4, 107–10, 169; and invisible labor, 40–43, 45, 50, 52, 58–59, 61, 138, 142–44; and resistance to WFOC, 17, 136, 140, 170–72; and teaching innovation,

71, 112–14, 119–20, 123, 126–27, 130–31, 133, 159; and teaching statements, 27–32; and time, 152, 154
reviews, teaching, 5, 7–8, 20, 63, 75, 107, 137; and classroom management, 37, 73–75; and diverse and multiple perspectives, 54–55, 98–99, 101, 103; and innovation, 112–13, 118–19, 127; and invisible labor, 139–40, 143; and joy, 135, 158
rewards, 42, 54, 84, 102–5, 107–8, 112–14, 131–32, 135, 159, 169; and students, 70–71

scholarship, 2, 7, 13, 19, 38, 63, 81–82, 96, 154, 172; and invisible labor, 139, 145. *See also* publications,
Scholarship of Teaching and Learning (SoTL), 6, 25–27, 31, 35–37; and classroom management, 64, 67, 75–81, 83, 88; and diverse and multiple perspectives, 93, 102–5, 108–9; and super-invisible teaching labor, 41, 45, 47–48, 50–51, 54–57, 59–60; and teaching innovation, 113–14, 118–20, 124–28, 130–32; and time, 149, 151, 155, 162. *See also* SoTL Minefields
science of learning, 120–21, 127–28, 132
self-care, 7–8, 156–57. *See also* protection
self-reflection, 2, 6–7, 13, 16, 29, 36–37, 82–84, 172; and diverse and multiple perspectives, 86, 91, 107, 109; and invisible labor, 139, 143; and joy, 135–36, 147–48; and teaching futures, 162–63; and teaching innovation, 116, 118, 133; and teaching statements, 45, 50, 57, 60; and time, 152–56
service, 2, 39–40, 42, 101, 106–9, 116, 161, 171. *See also* advising; committees; mentoring
sexism, 92, 101, 133, 140, 147, 149

silencing, 3, 20, 95, 100–101, 103, 131, 170
society, contributions to, 15–17, 35, 47–50, 55, 102, 105
SoTL Minefields, 10; and assumptions about power, 32–35; and classroom management, 75–81, 170; and diverse and multiple perspectives, 102–4; and learning outcomes, 52–57; and super-invisible labor, 146–47; and teaching innovation, 130
stereotypes, 49, 77–78. *See also* myths, teaching
strategic actions, 9–10, 37, 136; and any and every threat, 22–29, 31–32; and burnout, 152–55, 158–60; and course content, 93–96, 104–8; and diverse and multiple perspectives, 104–9; student incivility, 63–71; and super-invisible teaching labor, 43–52; and teaching and assessment methods 120–30; and teaching overwhelm 43–57; and teaching statements, 22–32; and time, 149–56, 161
stress, 2, 4, 66, 73–74, 97, 103, 145, 150, 156, 159–60
students, 6, 15–16; and classroom management, 64–84; of color, 2, 48, 143–44; and diverse and multiple perspectives, 44–50, 87–95, 98–99, 101–10; and invisible labor, 39–43, 59–60, 139–45, 147; and joy, 135, 158–60, 162; and negative interactions, 5, 7, 13, 17, 18, 61–63, 77, 79, 112, 136–37, 141–42, 162; and privilege, 33–35, 57; and resistance to WFOC, 17–21, 23, 57; and teaching, 23–30, 32, 36, 54–56, 111–33; and time, 138, 146, 148–60, 163. *See also* assessment, learning; classrooms; disruptions, classroom; incivilities; learning, student; participation, student; reviews, teaching

success, 11, 19, 52, 112–13, 136, 145, 147–48, 152–55, 158, 171–73; and joy, 159, 161–63; and teaching, 72, 105, 123, 131, 142
super-invisible labor, 40–52, 54–57, 58–60, 139, 146–47
syllabi, 23, 28, 67, 72, 91, 110, 151

teaching, 1–4, 6, 8–13, 16, 19–20, 146–47; and classroom management, 63–67, 70–76, 78, 80–84; and diverse and multiple perspectives, 21–22, 46–57, 88, 91–110; and innovation, 111–33; and invisible labor, 38–45, 58–62, 134–45; and joy, 158–63; and labor, 52, 94, 104, 109, 146–63; and observation, 54, 63, 118, 143, 171; and teaching loads, 5, 7, 42, 64, 74, 138, 142, 172; and teaching statements, 23–37, 58; and time, 149–56. See also learning, student; pedagogy; Scholarship of Teaching and Learning (SoTL); SoTL Minefields; teaching and learning centers; teaching excellence, WFOC
teaching and learning centers, 3, 6, 128, 130, 172
teaching excellence, WFOC, 10, 12, 14–18, 29–30, 35–36, 117; and diverse and multiple perspectives, 84–90, 108, 110; and innovation, 114–16, 119, 122, 128, 131, 133, 159; and invisible labor, 41–42, 44–45, 50, 59–60, 144, 149; and privilege, 53–54; and SoTL, 57–58
tenure, 2, 4–5, 7–9, 13, 17, 147, 163; and classroom management, 73–74, 84; and diverse and multiple perspectives, 91, 99, 101, 103, 109–10; and invisible labor, 39–43, 45, 50–51, 55–56, 59–60, 139; and resistance to WFOC, 19–20, 22; and teaching innovation, 112–13, 119–20, 130–33, 135, 137, 139; and teaching statements, 29, 31, 36–37 and time, 151, 154. See also promotion
tenure credit/currency, 19, 40–45, 50, 52
threats, career, 4–9, 13, 31, 52, 157; any and every threat 16–20; assessing, 135–56; and burnout 136–45; and classroom management, 72–75, 78–79, 82; and course content 90–93; and diverse and multiple perspectives, 87, 90–93, 96, 101, 103–4, 106; student incivility 72–75; and teaching, 114, 118–20, 143; and teaching and assessment methods 118–20; teaching overwhelm 39–41
thriving, 2–3, 21–22, 34–35, 65–66, 83, 131, 135, 147, 161; and teaching innovation, 87, 90, 99, 102, 104. See also flourishing
time, 4, 7, 10, 15, 19, 127, 145, 172; and joy, 160, 163; and management, 64, 66, 74, 84; and self-care, 156–57; and teaching, 24, 38, 40–41, 138, 148–56
toxicity, 74–75, 81–83, 149, 155–56

vision statements, institutional, 16–17, 104
visualization, 2–3, 7, 37, 63, 135

well-being, 9, 49, 52, 73, 81–82, 144, 154, 158, 160. See also emotional well-being; mental well-being; physical well-being
worldviews, 48, 91, 93, 98, 141. See also mainstream perspectives

TEACHING, ENGAGING, AND THRIVING IN HIGHER ED SERIES

James M. Lang and Michelle D. Miller, Series Editors

Other books in the series:

A Pedagogy of Kindness
Catherine J. Denial

A Teacher's Guide to Learning Student Names:
Why You Should, Why It's Hard, How You Can
Michelle D. Miller

The Present Professor:
Authenticity and Transformational Teaching
Elizabeth A. Norell

The Opposite of Cheating:
Teaching for Integrity in the Age of AI
Tricia Bertram Gallant and David A. Rettinger

Making Writing Meaningful:
A Guide for Higher Education
Michele Eodice, Anne Ellen Geller, and Neal Lerner

Snafu Edu:
Teaching and Learning When Things Go Wrong in the College Classroom
Jessamyn Neuhaus

www.ingramcontent.com/pod-product-compliance
Lightning Source LLC
Chambersburg PA
CBHW032251150426
43195CB00008BA/413